# LIGHT AIRCRAFT RECOGNITION

## THIRD EDITION

## PETER R. MARCH

PLYMOUTH PRESS

IAN ALLAN
*Publishing*

# CONTENTS

First published 1992
Reprinted 1993
Second edition 1995
Third edition 1997

ISBN 1-882663-15-2

Co-published by Plymouth Press Ltd and Ian Allan Ltd.
Distributed in the United States by Plymouth Press Ltd,
101 Panton Road, Vergennes, VT 05491.
For a free catalog of Plymouth Press books and products call (800) 477-2398 or (802) 877-2150.

Printed in Great Britain

## ACKNOWLEDGEMENTS

The author would like to thank Brian Strickland for the detailed research and preparation of the material, Ben Dunnell for checking the copy and Jean Strickland for typing the text.

## PHOTOGRAPHS

Most of the copyright illustrations in *abc Light Aircraft Recognition* are from the PRM Aviation Photo Library, as credited: Andrew March (APM), Daniel March (DJM), Peter R. March (PRM) and Brian Strickland (BSS). Additional photographs as credited.

*Front cover:* **Extra EA300s of Firebird Aerobatic Team.** *PRM*
*Back cover:* **De Havilland Dragon Fly and de Havilland Dragon Rapide.** *PRM*

# INTRODUCTION

This revised third edition of *abc Light Aircraft Recognition* has again been produced in series with *abc Civil Airliner Recognition, abc Biz Jets: Business and Corporate Aircraft* and *abc Classic & Warbird Recognition* and is a companion to *abc Civil Aircraft Markings*. The title 'Light Aircraft' also includes light helicopters that have not been included in the above titles. These are now grouped into a separate section, so that comparisons can be made more readily.

The book's aim is to provide a recognition guide to some of the diverse types of civilian-operated light aircraft, from the tiny ARV Super 2 to the aerobatic Zlin, likely to be seen at airports and airfields. Space does not permit the inclusion of many homebuilt aircraft designs, nor those types or variants seldom seen at provincial airports.

The aircraft are presented in the established *abc* 'Recognition Series' format, under the individual heading of the design company and/or principal manufacturer followed by the aircraft's category and the name of the variant for which the detailed description is then given. Standard headings are used to provide data on the aircraft's powerplant, dimensions, speed and accommodation. Where known, the first flight date of the prototype or the variant(s) marked is shown, followed by an indication of the number of the type produced. The key recognition features of the aircraft are then described, concluding with a list of the main variants of the type, with brief information as to how they vary one from another. Photographs are shown with each type of aircraft to help with recognition. This is repeated for light helicopters.

After the detailed presentations, further brief descriptions are provided covering a selection of homebuilt types and some company-manufactured aircraft, like the Christen Eagle and Yak-18, that are present only in relatively small numbers, but which should be included as significant light aircraft. To assist in locating specific aircraft by name and/or manufacturer, a comprehensive index and cross-reference has also been provided.

# AUTHOR

Peter R. March is also author of the following publications:
*abc Combat Aircraft Recognition* (Ian Allan 1992)
*abc Civil Airliner Recognition* (Ian Allan 1995)
*abc Classic & Warbird Recognition* (Ian Allan 1996)
*abc Biz Jets* (Ian Allan 1996)
*abc Military Aircraft Markings* (Ian Allan 1997)
*Royal Air Force Almanac* (RAFBFE 1994)
*Hawk Comes of Age* (RAFBFE 1995)
*The Real Aviation Enthusiast II* (RAFBFE 1995)
and is Managing Editor of the *Royal Air Force Yearbook* series (RAF Benevolent Fund Enterprises).

# PERFORMANCE ABBREVIATIONS

| | | | |
|---|---|---|---|
| ehp | equivalent horsepower | kW | kilowatt |
| eshp | equivalent shaft horsepower | mph | miles per hour |
| hp | horsepower | shp | shaft horsepower |
| km/h | kilometers per hour | st | static thrust |

## Aeronca 7AC/ACA
Single-engined high-wing light aircraft
Basic data for Aeronca 7AC Champion
*Powerplant:* One 65hp (48.4kW) Continental A65-8 piston engine
*Span:* 35ft 2in (10.72m)
*Length:* 21ft 6in (6.55m)
*Max cruising speed:* 85mph (137km/h)
*Accommodation:* Pilot plus one passenger, in tandem
*First aircraft flown:* May 1944
*Production:* 7AC – 7200; 7ACA – 71; 7BCM (L-16A) – 509; 7DC – 184; 7EC – 773; 11AC – 1867
*Recognition:* High-wing monoplane. Wing of parallel chord and rounded tips. V-wing struts from lower fuselage over landing gear legs. Fixed undercarriage without wheel spats, with cross bracing between wheels. Rounded fin and rudder. Relatively deep glazed cockpit with tandem seating. Pronounced curving of rear side glazing.
*Variants:* **Aeronca 7BC Champion** had a fuel-injected 85hp (63.5kW) Continental O-191-1 or 90hp (67kW) O-205-1 engine and featured a transparent roof and jettisonable doors; the **7DC** had the 65hp (48.4kW) or 85hp (63.5kW) Continental engine and **7EC** a 90hp (67kW) Continental C90-12. **Aeronca 11AC Chief** was generally similar except for increased fuselage width to accommodate side-by-side seating and a lower cowling line to give improved visibility. The **7ACA** was an updated 7AC reintroduced in 1971 with Franklin 2A-120B engine. The **7DCS** is a floatplane version.

*Above:* Aeronca 7BCM Champion. *DJM*

*Right:* Aeronca 11AC Chief. *BSS*

## ARV Super 2

Two-seat light aircraft
Basic data for ARV Super 2
*Powerplant:* One 77hp (57.4kW)
    Mid-West Aero-Engines AE75
    three-cylinder 750cc two-stroke
    engine
*Span:* 28ft 6in (8.69m)
*Length:* 18ft 0in (5.49m)
*Max cruising speed:* 104mph (167km/h)
*Accommodation:* Two seats
*First aircraft flown:* 11 March 1985
*Production:* 28 initially by ARV on Isle of Wight

*Top and Above:* ARV Super 2.
*PRM*

*Recognition:* Shoulder-wing monoplane with front stagger to leading edge of
    wings. Fixed tricycle undercarriage. Single strut to wing from top of
    undercarriage leg. Side-by-side seating in large glazed canopy. Built from
    supral light alloy which permits multi-curvature panels. Single fin and rudder
    with square-cut top. Long dorsal fillet. Pronounced air intakes immediately
    behind spinner.
*Variants:* From 1991 new powerplants being fitted — including Rotax and
    Norton Rotary engines. **Series 100** — basic trainer; **Series 200** — increased
    take-off weight and range; **Series 300** — 90hp Norton Rotary engine; **Series
    400** — 90hp Rotary engine and increased take-off weight; **Series 500** — as
    Series 300, but cleared for aerobatics. In 1993, ASL set up a joint venture
    company — ASL Hagfors Aero AB — to build the Super 2 at Hagfors, Sweden.
    It is now retitled Opus 280 and fitted with a Rotax 912A engine.

# Auster/Beagle Series
Single-engined high-wing light aircraft
Basic data for Auster J/1N Alpha
*Powerplant:* One 130hp (97kW) Gipsy Major I piston engine
*Span:* 36ft 0in (10.98m)
*Length:* 23ft 5in (7.14m)
*Max cruising speed:* 100mph (161km/h)
*Accommodation:* Pilot plus two/three seats
*First aircraft flown:* J/1 Autocrat 7 March 1946
*Production:* All Auster variants 3,741
*Recognition:* Most of the series are externally similar. Engine and tail shapes differ slightly. All have V-strut wing bracing and parallel chord wings. Fixed taildragger undercarriage.
*Variants:* **D/1 Auster Mk1** — developed from Taylorcraft Plus D; **E Auster Mk3** — 130hp (96.9kW) Gipsy Major I and flaps; **G Auster Mk4** — 130hp (96.9kW) Lycoming O-290-3 engine; **J Auster Mk5** — civil production Mk5; **Auster J/2 Arrow** — side-by-side two-seater with 75hp (55.9kW) Continental C75-12 and no flaps; **J/1 Autocrat** — three-seat civil model based on Mk5 with Blackburn Cirrus Minor; **J/1 Alpha** — 130hp (96.9kW) Gipsy Major I and enlarged fin/rudder; **J/1B Aiglet** — 130hp (96.9kW) Gipsy Major I, wider fuselage and reduced wingspan; **J/5B Autocar** — four-seat J/1 with 130hp (96.9kW) Gipsy Major I, high-back rear fuselage; **J/5F Aiglet Trainer** — two-seat trainer version of J/1B with clipped wings; **Auster AOP6** — 145hp (108.13kW) Gipsy Major VII (also Beagle Terrier); **Auster AOP9** — 180hp (134.2kW) Cirrus Bombardier 203 engine, single wing struts; **D5 Husky** — either 160hp (119.3kW) Lycoming O-320A or 180hp (134.2kW) Lycoming O-360-A2A, new fin and rudder.

**Auster J/1N Alpha.** *DJM*

## BA Swallow/Klemm

Single-engined two-seat light aircraft
Basic data for British Aircraft Manufacturing Company (BA) Swallow II
*Powerplant:* One 80hp (59.7kW) Pobjoy Cataract II radial or 75hp (56kW)
    British Salmson
*Span:* 42ft 8.5 in (13.03m)
*Length:* 27ft 0in (8.23m)
*Max cruising speed:* 92mph (148km/h)
*Accommodation:* Pilot plus one passenger
*First aircraft flown:* 1935
*Production:* Originally known as British Klemm, the BA Swallow was a
    licence-built Klemm L25
*Recognition:* Tandem open cockpit low-wing monoplane. Long tapered wings
    with square tips. Exposed engine cylinders with long single exhaust on
    starboard side. Fixed undercarriage and tail skid. Pronounced 'ribbing' on
    wings and fuselage.
*Variants:* The **BA Eagle** (Klemm L32) was a three-seat cabin monoplane version
    with a 130hp (97kW) de Havilland Gipsy Major or 185hp (138kW) Gipsy
    Six engine.

*Above:* **BA Swallow 2 (Pobjoy
Niagara 3).** *PRM*

*Right:* **BA Swallow 2 (Cirrus Minor).**
*PRM*

# Beagle A.109 Airedale

Single-engined four-seat light aircraft
Basic data for Beagle A.109 Airedale
*Powerplant:* One 180hp (130.7kW) Lycoming O-360-A1A piston engine
*Span:* 36ft 4in (11.07m)
*Length:* 26ft 4in (8.02m)
*Max cruising speed:* 133mph (214km/h)
*Accommodation:* Pilot plus three passengers
*First aircraft flown:* 16 April 1961
*Production:* 43
*Recognition:* High-wing monoplane. Wing of parallel chord and rounded tips. V-wing struts from lower fuselage under windscreen. Fixed tricycle undercarriage with wheel spats. Swept fin and rudder with dorsal fillet. Tapered tailplane set at base of rudder. Clean cowled engine.
*Variants:* **A.111** — 175hp (130.5kW) Continental GO-300 engine.

**Left and below:**
**Beagle A.109 Airedale.** *PRM*

# Beagle B.121 Pup

Two/three-seat leisure/aerobatic light aircraft
Basic data for Beagle Pup 150
*Powerplant:* One 150hp (112kW) Lycoming O-320-A2B piston engine
*Span:* 31ft 0in (9.45m)
*Length:* 23ft 2in (7.07m)
*Max cruising speed:* 131mph (211km/h)
*Accommodation:* Pilot plus one to three passengers
*First aircraft flown:* 8 April 1967
*Production:* 176
*Recognition:* Single-engined low-wing monoplane. Fixed tricycle undercarriage.
   Short nose. Large glazed area to cabin with two windows each side. Tapered
   wings with square tips. Large fin and rudder and ventral strake under fin.
   Oblong tailplane with square tips set at base of fin.
*Variants:* **B.121 Pup 100** — original two-seat trainer with 100hp (74.57kW)
   Continental O-200-A engine; **B.121C Pup 150B** — four-seat tourer with
   150hp (112kW) Lycoming O-320-A2B; **Bulldog** — two-seat
   military trainer version with
   larger wing, sliding bubble
   cockpit and 200hp (149kW)
   Lycoming IO-360-A1B6 engine,
   first flown 19 May 1969.

*Right and below:*
**Beagle B.121 Pup 2.** *DJM/PRM*

## Beagle B.206 Bassett

Twin-engined four-seat light business aircraft
Basic data for Beagle B.206S
*Powerplant:* Two 340hp (260kW) Rolls-Royce Continental GT SIO-520-C
turbocharged piston engines
*Span:* 45ft 9.5in (13.95m)
*Length:* 33ft 8in (10.26m)
*Max cruising speed:* 187mph (301.6km/h)
*Accommodation:* Five/eight
*First aircraft flown:* 15 August 1961
Production: 72 of combined B.206 series, including 20 for the RAF
(as Basset CC1)
*Recognition:* Twin-engined low-wing monoplane. Straight leading edge to
wing, with tapering trailing edge leading to small square tips. Engine
nacelles entirely ahead of wing. Retractable tricycle undercarriage. Three
windows on each side of the fuselage. Swept fin and rudder. Tailplane set
low on fuselage extremity.
*Variants:* **B.206C** known as Beagle 206 Series 1. **B.206R** was the Basset CC1 for
the RAF. **B.206** Srs 3 was a 10-seat version with deeper fuselage and
longer cabin.

*Above:* Beagle B.206R. DJM

*Right:* Beagle B.206R. PRM

# Beech Model 17 Staggerwing

Single-engined four-seat cabin biplane
Basic data for Beech Model G17S Staggerwing
Powerplant: One 450hp (335.5kW) Pratt & Whitney R-985-AN-4 radial engine
*Span:* 32ft 0in (9.75m)
*Length:* 25ft 9in (7.84m)
*Max cruising speed:* 198mph (319km/h)
*Accommodation:* Pilot plus three passengers
*First aircraft flown:* 4 November 1932
*Production:* Most of the production was prewar but some 70 civil G17S were
produced in the late 1940s. Some 200 are still on the American register.
*Recognition:* Single-engined biplane. Wings, with rounded tips,
of backward stagger. Large radial engine, with two-blade propeller. Inwards
retracting main wheels. Upper wing is immediately above cabin. Single strut
between wings. Upright leading edge to tail fin with curved trailing edge.
*Variants:* None in the postwar production series.

***Above and left:* Beech D-17S
Staggerwing. *PRM***

# Beechcraft 23/24 Musketeer/Sundowner/Sierra/Sport

Four/six-seat all-metal light aircraft
Basic data for Beech Sierra 200
*Powerplant:* One 200hp (149kW) Lycoming IO-360-A1B6 piston engine
*Span:* 32ft 9in (9.98m)
*Length:* 25ft 9in (7.85m)
*Max* cruising speed: 158mph (254km/h)
*Accommodation:* Pilot plus three/five passengers
*First aircraft flown:* 23 October 1961 (Musketeer)
*Production:* 4,556
*Recognition:* Single-engined low-wing monoplane with retractable tricycle
   undercarriage. Wings of parallel chord with square tips. Oblong tailplane set
   low on rear fuselage. Swept fin and rudder with dorsal fin fairing. Four
   windows on each side. Short nose.
*Variants:* **A23 Musketeer** — four-seat with fixed undercarriage and 160hp
   (119kW) Lycoming O-320-B engine; **Sundowner 180** — with 180hp (134kW)
   Lycoming O-360-A4K; **Sierra 200** — four/six-seater with retractable
   undercarriage and 200hp (149kW) injected engine; **Sport 150** — 150hp
   (112kW) two-seat aerobatic version.

*Left:* **Beechcraft A23 Musketeer.**
*PRM*

*Below:* **Beechcraft 19A Musketeer**
**Sport.** *PRM*

*Above:* **Beechcraft F33C Bonanza.**
*PRM*

*Right:* **Beechcraft 35 Bonanza.** *PRM*

# Beechcraft 33/35/36 Bonanza/Debonair

Single-engined four/five-seat executive aircraft
Basic data for Beech Model F33A Bonanza
*Powerplant:* One 285hp (212kW) Lycoming IO-520-BB piston engine
*Span:* 33ft 6in (10.21m)
*Length:* 26ft 8in (8.13m)
*Max cruising speed:* 198mph (319km/h)
*Accommodation:* Pilot plus three/four passengers
*First aircraft flown:* 22 December 1945 (35); 4 September 1959 (C33)
*Production:* 13,901
*Recognition:* Single-engine low-wing monoplane with retractable tricycle
  undercarriage. Straight wing leading edge with tapered trailing edge.
  Rounded wing tips. Four cabin windows on each side. Upright fin and rudder
  with square top. Dorsal fin fairing from rear of cabin. Conventional tailplane
  set midway. Original Model 35 Bonanza had a V-tail.
*Variants:* **C33/F33A** — originally known as the Debonair until 1967. Now
  known as Bonanza and has conventional tail system; **F33C** — aerobatic
  version; **35** — V-tail original production version; **A36** — lengthened version
  to make full six-seater with 300hp (223kW) Continental IO-520-BB engine;
  **A36TC** – turbocharged version of A36; **B36TC** – span increased
  to 37ft 10in (11.53m).

## Beechcraft 76 Duchess
Twin-engined light transport aircraft
Basic data for Beech 76 Duchess
*Powerplant:* Two 180hp (130.7kW) Lycoming O-360-A1G6D piston engines
*Span:* 38ft 0in (11.58m)
*Length:* 29ft 0in (8.86m)
*Max cruising speed:* 191mph (308km/h)
*Accommodation:* Pilot plus three passengers
*First aircraft flown:* 24 May 1977
*Production:* 437
*Recognition:* Twin-engined low-wing monoplane with retractable tricycle
    undercarriage. Wings of parallel chord with square tips. Fairing at front wing
    root. Engines mounted high on wing leading edge. Swept oblong fin and
    rudder with dorsal fairing, square tips and T-tail. Three cabin windows on
    each side. Doors on both sides.
*Variants:* None.

*Left:* Beechcraft 76 Duchess. *PRM*

*Below:* Beechcraft 76 Duchess. *BSS*

*Above and right:*
**Boeing Stearman A75.** *PRM*

# Boeing Stearman/Kaydet

Single-engined two-seat biplane trainer
Basic data for Stearman 75 series PT-17 Kaydet
*Powerplant:* One 220hp (164.2kW) Continental R-670-5 radial piston engine
*Span:* 32ft 2in (9.80m)
*Length:* 24ft 10in (7.54m)
*Max cruising speed:* 106mph (171km/h)
*Accommodation:* Two seats in tandem open cockpits
*First aircraft flown:* 1934
*Production:* 10,000+
*Recognition:* Large seven-cylinder radial engine with exposed cylinders. Biplane
   of equal length, parallel chord and rounded tips. Cantilever main
   undercarriage in taildragger configuration usually without wheel spats. Twin
   open cockpits. Pointed fin with curved trailing edge to rudder. Braced
   tapered tailplane.
*Variants:* **A75N1** — with 225hp (167.8kW) Jacobs R-755-7 radial engine. Some
   aircraft have been adapted to take larger powerplants such as the 450hp
   (335.6kW) Pratt & Whitney engine.

# Bolkow Bo 208 Junior

Single-engined two-seat light aircraft
Basic data for Bo 208C Junior
*Powerplant:* One 100hp (74.5kW) Rolls-Royce Continental O-200-A
   piston engine
*Span:* 26ft 4in (8.02m)
*Length:* 19ft 0in (5.79m)
*Max cruising speed:* 127mph (205km/h)
*Accommodation:* Two side-by-side seats
*First aircraft flown:* 1958
*Production:* 200+

*Recognition:* Single-engine shoulder-wing monoplane. Slight forward stagger
   to front leading edge of wings. Single strut wing braces. Fixed tricycle
   undercarriage. Short nose. Small glazed area to cockpit. Low set rectangular
   tailplane behind slim swept fin and rudder.

*Variants:* **MFI-9 Junior** — initial Swedish version; **MFI-9 Trainer** — trainer,
   including military version; **MFI-15** — updated trainer version; **Bo 208 Junior**
   — production by Bolkow in Germany.

*Above:* **Bolkow Bo 208A2 Junior.**
**PRM**

*Right:* **Bolkow Bo 208C Junior.**
**DJM**

# Brügger MB-2 Colibri 2

Single-seat homebuilt monoplane
Basic data for Brügger MB-2 Colibri 2
*Powerplant:* One 40hp (30kW) 1,600cc Volkswagen (Brügger modification)
  piston engine
*Span:* 19ft 8.25in (6.0m)
*Length:* 15ft 9in (4.80m)
*Max cruising speed:* 99mph (160km/h)
*Accommodation:* Pilot only
*First aircraft flown:* 1 May 1970
*Production:* Some 280 are under construction or flying in Europe
*Recognition:* Single-engined low-wing monoplane. No fixed fin. Non-
  retractable tailwheel landing gear — main wheels usually have spats. Wings
  of equal chord and taper with square tips. Domed perspex canopy. Bulged
  covers on each side of nose for engine valve gear.
*Variants:* None.

***Above and right:* Brügger MB2
Colibri. *PRM***

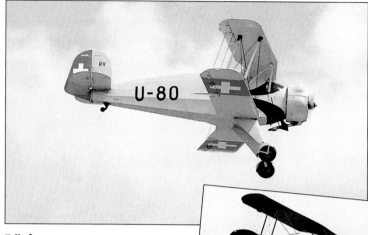

## Bücker
## Jungmann/Jungmeister

Light two-seat biplane trainer
Basic data for Bücker Bü 131B Jungmann
*Powerplant:* One 105hp (78.2kW) Hirth
 HM504A-2 piston engine (Jungmann);
 160hp (119kW) Siemens Sh.14A piston
 engine (Jungmeister)
*Span:* 24ft 4in (7.40m)
*Length:* 21ft 9in (6.62m)
*Max cruising speed:* 106mph (170km/h)
*Accommodation:* Pilot plus one passenger
*First aircraft flown:* 27 April 1934

**Top: Bücker Bü 133D
Jungmeister.** *DJM*

**Above: Bücker/CASA 1.131E
Jungmann.** *PRM*

*Production:* Mass production in Germany as a trainer and used in 21 countries.
 Also licence-built in Czechoslovakia, Holland, Spain and Switzerland. (A total
 of 55 Jungmanns were produced by CASA in Spain in the 1950s.)
*Recognition:* Tandem two-seat cockpit (Jungmann). Single-seat
 (Jungmeister). Equal span, single-bay biplane with moderate sweep back and
 rounded tips. Slight dihedral on lower plane. Fixed undercarriage, with cross
 bracing and pronounced forward-sweep undercarriage legs. Upright leading
 edge to fin and rounded tip.
*Variants:* **Bü 131A Jungmann** was fitted with 80hp (59.6kW) Hirth HM60R
 engine and **Bü 131B** a 105hp (78.2kW) Hirth inverted engine. **Bü 133C**
 Jungmeister was a single-seat advanced trainer. The **Bü 133DI** had an Sh.14
 A4 engine and **Bü 133F** had a 220hp (164kW) Franklin 6A-350-C1 engine.
 These classic prewar aerobatic aircraft are now available again in kit form,
 using original jigs, produced by Bücker Prado in California.

# CAARP/Mudry CAP-10/20/21/230

Training, touring, aerobatic aircraft
Basic data for CAARP CAP-10B
*Powerplant:* One 180hp (134kW) Textron Lycoming AEIO-360-B2F piston engine
*Span:* 26ft 5in (8.06m)
*Length:* 23ft 6in (7.16m)
*Max cruising speed:* 155mph (250km/h)
*Accommodation:* Pilot plus one passenger
*First aircraft flown:* 22 August 1968 (CAP-10)
*Production:* CAP-10B — 268+; CAP-20/A/B — 21; CAP-21/230 — 27. Series
  production continuing; CAP- 231EX – 6
*Recognition:* Low-wing monoplane with square-tipped, slightly elliptical wings.
  Wide-track undercarriage with forward single strutted legs and wheel spats.
  Domed perspex canopy. Large square-tipped fin and rudder. Tail-plane set
  high on rear fuselage forward of rudder. Bulbous cover over exhaust
  manifolds.
*Variants:* **CAP-10B** — production version of CAP-10 derived from Piel CP301;
  **CAP-20** — single-seat competition aerobatic derivative; **CAP-21** — cantilever
  undercarriage and redesigned wings; **CAP-230** — with 300hp (223.7kW)
  Lycoming AEIO-54-L1 engine and angular tail; **CAP-231** — single-seat
  competition aerobatic aircraft; **CAP-231 EX** — export version, with carbon
  fibre components including the wing built by Walter Extra. **CAP-232** — with
  new Mudry-designed carbon fibre wing with thinner section and
  modified ailerons.

*Above and left:*
**CAARP/Mudry CAP-231.** *PRM*

## Cessna 120/140/170

Single-engined two-seat light aircraft
Basic data for Cessna 140
*Powerplant:* One 85hp (63.4kW) Continental C85-12F piston engine
*Span:* 32ft 10in (10.0m)
*Length:* 21ft 6in (6.55m)
*Max cruising speed:* 105mph (169km/h)
*Accommodation:* Two side-by-side seats
*First aircraft flown:* 28 June 1945 (120/140); September 1947 (170)
*Production:* Cessna 120 — 2,171; Cessna 140 — 4,907; Cessna 140A — 525;
     Cessna 170 — 5,173
*Recognition:* Single-engined high-wing monoplane. V-bracing to wings from
     top of undercarriage leg. Wings of parallel chord and rounded tips.
     Taildragger configuration undercarriage. Rounded fin and rudder. Low-set
     tapered tailplane.
*Variants:* **120** — an economy model of 140 without flaps; **140** — main
     production version with metal/fabric wings and flaps. Powered by 85hp
     (63.4kW) Continental C85-12 or 12F engine; **140A** — all-metal wings and
     Continental C-90-12 engine; **170** — four-seat development as an enlarged
     140 with 145hp (108.1kW) Continental C-145.

*Above:* Cessna 120. *PRM*

*Right:* Cessna 140A. *PRM*

## Cessna 150/152 Aerobat
Single-engined two-seat training aircraft
Basic data for Cessna 152
*Powerplant:* One 108hp (82.0kW) Lycoming O-235-N2C piston engine
*Span:* 32ft 8in (9.97m)
*Length:* 24ft 1in (7.34m)
*Max cruising speed:* 122mph (196km/h)
*Accommodation:* Pilot plus one passenger/student
*First aircraft flown:* 15 September 1957
*Production:* Cessna 150 — 23,751; Cessna 152 — 7,584
*Recognition:* Single-engined high-wing monoplane. Fixed tricycle
    undercarriage. One main window (in-door) on each side with rear window
    behind wing. Single strut bracing to wing. Straight wing leading edge with
    square tips. Swept fin and rudder with small dorsal fin fairing.
    Low-set tailplane.
*Variants:* Cessna **150A**, **B** and **C** were early production models with vertical tail-
    fin and built-up top fuselage and 100hp (74.6kW) Continental engine; **150D**
    — introduced wrap-around rear window; **150F** — first with swept fin and
    rudder; **A150K** — an aerobatic version with wider-track main undercarriage;
    **152** — more powerful 108hp (82.0kW)
    engine fitted. All production models
    built by Reims Aviation in France
    have prefix 'F' (eg F/152) and are
    powered by Rolls-Royce
    Continental engines.

**Above: Cessna 152. *PRM***

**Right: Reims Cessna F.150L. *PRM***

# Cessna 172 Skyhawk

All-metal four-seat piston-engined touring/ training aircraft
Basic data for Cessna 172P Skyhawk II
*Powerplant:* One 160hp (119kW) Lycoming O-320-D2J piston engine
*Span:* 35ft 10in (10.92m)
*Length:* 26ft 11in (8.20m)
*Max cruising speed:* 138mph (222km/h)
*Accommodation:* Pilot plus three passengers
*First aircraft flown:* 1955
*Production:* 35,773 (including 2,133 French-built F172s). In addition 237 military
  Mescaleros were built. Production recommenced at Independence, Kansas
  and first delivered November 1996. Initial models will be trainers.
*Recognition:* High-wing monoplane with single thick wing braces under leading
  edge. Slightly tapered wings with squared tips. Tricycle undercarriage often
  featuring wheel spats. Swept fin and rudder with small dorsal fillet at front
  of fin. Tailplane set low at rear extremity.
*Variants:* **Cessna 172** — a development of the 170 with a tricycle
  undercarriage; **172A** — revised swept tail; **172B** — deeper fuselage; **172D** —
  cut-down rear fuselage; **172E** — 150hp (111.8kW) Continental O-300; **172I** —
  150hp (111.8kW) Lycoming O-320-E2D; **172N** — 160hp (119.3kW) Lycoming
  O-320-H2AD; **172Q** — 180hp (134.2kW) Lycoming O-360-A4N; **FR172 Reims
  Rocket** — 210hp (156.6kW) Continental IO-360-D; **R172K Hawk XPII** —
  172N with 195hp Continental IO-360-K; **Skyhawk** — de luxe version of the
  172; **175 Skylark** — powered by 175hp (130.5kW) Continental GO-300-E;
  **172RG Cutlass** — more powerful 180hp (134.2kW) Lycoming O-360-A4N
  engine and retractable undercarriage.

**Reims Cessna F.172N Skyhawk II.** *PRM*

# Cessna 177 Cardinal

Cessna 177RG Cardinal. *DJM*

Single-engined light aircraft
Basic data for Cessna 177B Cardinal II
*Powerplant:* One 180hp (134kW) Lycoming O-360-A1F6 piston engine
*Span:* 35ft 6in (10.82m)
*Length:* 27ft 3in (8.31m)
*Max cruising speed:* 150mph (241km/h)
*Accommodation:* Four seats. Optional seat for two children aft of rear seats
*First aircraft flown:* 15 July 1966 (177); 16 February 1970 (177RG)
*Production:* 4,294 (including Reims-built F177RG)
*Recognition:* Single-engined high-wing monoplane. Straight leading edge to
   wing with tapering trailing edge, cambered tips but no wing struts. Tricycle
   undercarriage which retracts on the RG model. Swept fin and rudder with
   dorsal fairing. Low-set oblong tailplane. Raked front windscreen.
*Variants:* **Cessna 177** — original model with fixed undercarriage and 150hp
   (111.8kW) Lycoming O-320-E2D engine. De luxe model has wheel spats; **177A**
   — with 180hp (134.2kW) Lycoming; **177B Cardinal II** — cambered wingtips
   and extra child seat. Constant speed prop; **177 Cardinal Classic** — de luxe
   version of 177B; **177RG/Cardinal** — with retractable undercarriage and
   200hp (149.1kW) Lycoming IO-360-A1B6D.

# Cessna 180/185 Skywagon/182 Skylane

Single-engined light aircraft
Basic data for Cessna 180
*Powerplant:* One 230hp (173kW) Continental O-470-A piston engine
*Span:* 35ft 10in (10.92m)
*Length:* 25ft 9in (7.85m)
*Max cruising speed:* 170mph (274km/h)
*Accommodation:* Pilot plus five passengers
*First aircraft flown:* 26 May 1952
*Production:* 6,000+ (180), 18,000+ (182); production of Cessna 182 resumed November 1996
*Recognition:* High-wing monoplane with a single wing brace to the lower edge of the fuselage. Squared wing, tailplane and fin tips. Tailwheel undercarriage with the low-pressure main wheels on sprung steel legs from the lower fuselage below the wing brace; tailwheel projects beyond the base of the fin. Pronounced dorsal fillet forward of the fin. Tailplane set low on the rear extremity of the fuselage.
*Variants:* **180 Skywagon II** — de luxe version of 180; **180A** — with 230hp (171.5kW) Continental O-470-L; **182 Skylane** — has a tricycle undercarriage and accommodation for four people; **182A** to **182R** — various changes in configuration and internal fit: **182C** first with swept fin and rudder; **182E** first with cut-down rear fuselage; **182P** larger dorsal fin; **F182 Skylanes** — built by Reims Aviation in France; **R182 Skylane RG** — with 235hp (175.2kW) Lycoming O-540-J3C5D and retractable undercarriage; **185 Skywagon** — development of the 180 with 300hp (223.7kW) Continental IO-520-D; **185 Skywagon II** — de luxe version.

**Cessna 182P Skylane.** *PRM*

## Cessna 206 Super Skywagon/207 Stationair 6

Single-engined six/seven-seat light aircraft
Basic data for Cessna U206G Stationair 6
*Powerplant:* One 300hp (224kW) Continental IO-520-F piston engine
*Span:* 35ft 10in (10.92m)
*Length:* 28ft 0in (8.61m)
*Max cruising speed:* 169mph (272km/h)
*Accommodation:* Pilot plus five passengers
*First aircraft flown:* 1962
*Production:* Cessna 206 — 7,508; Cessna 207 — 788; production of Cessna 206 resumed November 1996
*Recognition:* Similar to the Cessna 182 but with extended glazed cabin area to seat six, longer fuselage and larger fin.
*Variants:* **U206 Super Skywagon** — more powerful engine and double cargo doors on the starboard side. Subsequently named Stationair (from U206F) and Stationair 6 (U206G); **207A Skywagon 207** — further extended (18in) fuselage and cabin to seat 7/8; **Turbo-Stationair 8** — eight-seat development of Stationair 7 with TSIO-520-M engine.

*Above:* **Cessna U206F Stationair.**
PRM

*Right:* **Cessna U206G Stationair 6.**
PRM

# Cessna 210 Centurion

Single-engined six-seat light aircraft
Basic data for Cessna 210L Centurion II
*Powerplant:* One 300hp (224kW)
  Continental IO-520-L six-cylinder
  piston engine
*Span:* 36ft 9in (11.20m)
*Length:* 28ft 2in (8.59m)
*Max cruising speed:* 193mph (311km/h)
*Accommodation:* Pilot plus five passengers in pairs
*First aircraft flown:* January 1957
*Production:* 9,336
*Recognition:* Single-engined high-wing monoplane with retractable tricycle
  undercarriage. Straight leading edge to wing with turned-down tips. No
  wing bracing. Three side cabin windows. Swept fin and rudder with dorsal
  fillet from cabin roof. Low-set tapered tailplane.
*Variants:* **Cessna 210** — initial four-seat version with 260hp Continental engine
  and strut-braced wings; **210A to K** — varied upgradings to cabin and
  engine size; **210L** — main production version, some with turbocharged
  engine (T prefix); **210M/N/R** — with 310hp Continental TSIO-520-R engine;
  **P210N** — turbocharged 210N 310hp (231.2kW) TSIO-520-AF engine with
  pressurised cabin with four windows each side; **P210R** — P210N with longer-
  span stabiliser, cambered wingtips and 325hp (242.3kW) Continental
  GTSIO-520-CE engine.

*Top:* **Cessna T210N Turbo Centurion.** *DJM*

*Above:* **Cessna T210G Turbo Centurion.** *PRM*

## Cessna 310/320 Skyknight/340

Cessna 340. *PRM*

Twin-engined four-seat light business aircraft
Basic data for Cessna 310Q
*Powerplant:* Two 285hp (212kW) Continental IO-520-M piston engines
*Span:* 36ft 11in (11.25m)
*Length:* 32ft 0in (9.74m)
*Max cruising speed:* 225mph (361km/h)
*Accommodation:* Pilot plus three passengers (310); plus four/five passengers
(320); plus five passengers (340)
*First aircraft flown:* 3 January 1953 (310)
*Production:* Cessna 310 — 7,069; Cessna 320 — 622; Cessna 340 — 1,298
*Recognition:* Low-wing twin with wingtip tanks. Engine nacelles protrude
behind trailing edge of wings. Pointed nose. Swept fin and rudder with small
dorsal fillet and small ventral fin. Engines mounted high on wing
leading edges.
*Variants:* **Cessna 310** — five seat twin with vertical, squared-off fin and
rudder; 240hp (178.9kW) Continental O-470-B engines; **Cessna 310D** —
introduced swept fin and rudder; **Cessna 310G** — six-seat version with extra
cabin window and new tip tanks; **Cessna 310R** — largest production version
with bulged rear cabin roof and rear-view window; extended nose for
baggage; **320 Skynight** — six-seat version of 310F with longer cabin, extra
side window and turbocharged engines; **340** — pressurised model with
Cessna 414 wing and 285hp (212.5kW) Continental TSIO-520-K engines (TSIO-
520-N in 340A); longer fuselage and small circular cabin windows. Port side
rear entry door.

## Cessna 337 Super Skymaster

Four/six-seat twin light touring/transport aircraft
Basic data for Cessna T337H Super Skymaster II
*Powerplant:* Two 225hp (168kW) Continental TSIO-360-H piston engines
*Span:* 38ft 2in (11.63m)
*Length:* 29ft 10in (9.09m)
*Max cruising speed:* 236mph (380km/h)
*Accommodation:* Pilot plus three/five passengers
*First aircraft flown:* 28 February 1961 (Cessna 336)
*Production:* 3,437
*Recognition:* Twin-engined 'push and pull' configuration, twin-boomed high-wing monoplane. Two wing struts under leading edge. Retractable undercarriage. Straight leading edge to wing. Twin swept fins and rudders with ventral extensions.
*Variants:* **336 Skymaster** — initial version with fixed tricycle undercarriage and two 195hp (145.4kW) Continental IO-360A engines; **337 Super Skymaster** — more powerful 210hp (156.6kW) IO-360-C engines, retractable undercarriage and internal improvements. Other refinements on 337A to F; **T/P337G/H Pressurised Skymasters** — smaller windows, new front windscreen, more powerful turbo supercharged engines; **337G** — main production model with IO-360-G engines and new wing braces; **FTB-337** — unpressurised STOL version, with high-lift flaps and built by Reims Aviation.

***Above and right:***
**Reims Cessna F.337F Super Skymaster.** *PRM*

## Champion (Bellanca) Citabria

Single-engined two-seat light aircraft
Basic data for Bellanca 7GCAA Citabria
*Powerplant:* One 150hp (112kW) Avco Lycoming O-320-A2D piston engine
*Span:* 33ft 5in (10.19m)
*Length:* 22ft 8in (6.91m)
*Max cruising speed:* 129mph (207km/h)
*Accommodation:* Two seats in tandem
*First aircraft flown:* 1 May 1964
*Production:* 3,190
*Recognition:* Single-engined high-wing monoplane. Wings of equal chord with rounded tips. Short nose and squat fuselage. Taildragger undercarriage with very short main wheels, with spats. V-bracing to wing. Tapered braced tailplane. Angular fin and rudder with square top.
*Variants:* **7ECA** — basic version with 115hp (85.7kW) Lycoming O-235-C1; **7GCAA** — with 150hp (111.8kW) engine; **7GCBC Scout** — utility and agricultural version; **7KCAB** — aerobatic version with provision for inverted flying; **8KCAB Decathlon** — unlimited aerobatic version with Lycoming AEIO-320-E1B engine; **Super Decathlon** — with 180hp (134kW) AE10-360-H1A engine.

*Above:* **Bellanca 7GCBC Citabria.**
*PRM*

*Right:* **Bellanca 7GCAA.** *PRM*

## De Havilland Canada DHC1 Chipmunk
Single-engined tandem-seat training aircraft
Basic data for DHC Chipmunk 21
*Powerplant:* One 145hp (108kW) Gipsy Major 10 Mk2 piston engine
*Span:* 34ft 4in (10.45m)
*Length:* 25ft 5in (7.75m)
*Max cruising speed:* 124mph (199km/h)
*Accommodation:* Two seats in tandem
*First aircraft flown:* 22 May 1946
*Production:* 1,283
*Recognition:* Single-engined low-wing monoplane with fixed taildragger
  undercarriage. Tapered wings with square tips. Sliding canopy cover. Typical
  'DH' fin and rudder. Tapered tailplane at fuselage extremity.
*Variants:* **Chipmunk 21** — civil production version; **Chipmunk 22** — RAF
  Chipmunk T10; **Chipmunk 22A** — with larger fuel tanks; **Chipmunk 23** —
  single-seat agricultural version. Canadian-built and Bristol Tourer
  versions feature one-piece blown
  canopy cover; **Supermunk** —
  Chipmunk 22 re-engined with a
  180hp (134kW) Avco Lycoming
  O-360-A4A for use as a glider tug.

*Top:* **DHC1 Chipmunk 22.** *BSS*

*Right:* **DHC1 Chipmunk 22A.** *PRM*

# De Havilland DH82A Tiger Moth

Single-engined two-seat biplane trainer
Basic data for DH82A Tiger Moth
*Powerplant:* One 130hp (97kW) de Havilland Gipsy Major I or 120hp (89.5kW)
  Gipsy III piston engine
*Span:* 29ft 4in (8.94m)
*Length:* 23ft 11in (7.29m)
*Max cruising speed:* 93mph (150km/h)
*Accommodation:* Two seats in tandem open cockpits
*First aircraft flown:* 26 October 1931
*Production:* 7,000+
*Recognition:* Biplane of equal span with slightly swept wings. Twin open
  cockpits with small windscreens. Fabric-covered fuselage and wings.
  Distinctive de Havilland-shaped fin and rudder.
*Variants:* The all-wood construction **DH82B Queen Bee** was built for the RAF
  as a radio-controlled target aircraft. The four-seat cabin Thruxton Jackaroo
  was constructed from ex-RAF Tiger Moths; **DH82C** — as DH82A, built in
  Canada with enclosed cockpits.

*Right and below:*
**DH82A Tiger Moth.** *PRM*

# Extra EA200/230/300

Single-engined aerobatic monoplane
Basic data for Extra EA300

*Powerplant:* One 300hp (223.5kW) Lycoming AEIO-540-L1B5/Ll piston engine
*Span:* 26ft 3in (8.0m)
*Length:* 23ft 4.5in (7.12m)
*Max cruising speed:* 205mph (330km/h)
*Accommodation:* Single-seat (230); two-seat in tandem (300)
*First aircraft flown:* 1983 (230); August 1988 (300); 2 April 1996 (200)
*Production:* 110+
*Recognition:* Single-engined mid-wing monoplane. Tailwheel fixed
   undercarriage. Cantilever main wheel undercarriage with wheel spats.
   Straight wing leading edge with square tips and tapering trailing edge. Long
   one-piece cockpit canopy. Square top to fin and rudder. Tapering tailplane
   with square tips.
*Variants:* Single-seat **Extra 230** with 230hp (171.5kW) Lycoming, also single-
   seat **Extra 260** with 260hp (193.9kW) Lycoming. Larger two-seat **Extra 300**
   has 300hp (223.5kW) Lycoming. **Extra EA300L** — two-seat aerobatic training
   aircraft; **Extra EA300S** — high performance single-seater with AEIO-540
   L1B5 engine; **Extra 200** — low purchase price model with Lycoming AEIO-
   360-AlE engine for aero clubs, flying schools and private operations; **Extra
   400** — a five-seater high-performance high-wing cabin monoplane with a
   T-tail and retractable undercarriage, first flew 4 April 1996.

**Extra EA300. *PRM***

# Fournier (Sportavia) RF-3/RF-4/RF-5

Single-engined light sporting aircraft training sailplane

Basic data for Sportavia Fournier RF-5

*Powerplant:* One 68hp (50.74kW) Sportavia-Limbach SL1700E Comet piston engine

*Span:* 45ft 1in (13.74m)

*Length:* 27ft 7in (8.41m)

*Max cruising speed:* 115mph (185km/h)

*Accommodation:* RF-4 — pilot only; RF-5 – pilot plus one passenger

*First aircraft flown:* 1963 (RF-3); January 1968 (RF-5)

*Production:* RF-3 — 95, RF-4 — 158, RF-5 — 233

*Recognition:* Long high-aspect ratio wings in typical sailplane-type style (though it is not a motorised glider). Single retractable mainwheel with outriders under wing tips. RF-4 has single-seat cockpit; the RF-5 tandem two-seat glazed cockpit.

*Variants:* **RF-4D** — single-seat version with 1200cc VW engine built by Sportavia; **RF-5 Tandem** — two-seat development of RF-4 with Limbach engine; **RF-5B** — RF-5 with longer wings and cut-down rear fuselage built by Sportavia and by Helwan (Egypt — 20 examples); **RF-5AJ1** — RF-5 built by Aero Jaen with 80hp (59.6kW) Limbach L2000-EO1.

**Above: Sportavia Fournier RF-4D.**
*PRM*

**Right: Sportavia Fournier RF-5B Sperber.** *PRM*

## Fuji FA200 Aero Subaru

Single-engined two/four-seat light aircraft
Basic data for Fuji FA200-180
*Powerplant:* One 180hp (130kW) Lycoming IO-360-B1B fuel-injected
  piston engine
*Span:* 30ft 11in (9.42m)
*Length:* 26ft 10in (8.17m)
*Max cruising speed:* 127mph (204km/h)
*Accommodation:* Pilot plus one/two/three passengers
*First aircraft flown:* 21 August 1965
*Production:* 274
*Recognition:* Single-engined low-wing monoplane. Wings of parallel chord with
  rounded tips. Rectangular tailplane with rounded tips set on top of fuselage
  at base of fin. Fixed tricycle undercarriage, sometimes with wheel spats. Short
  nose, domed unglazed roof to cockpit roof. Swept fin and rudder.
*Variants:* **FA200-160** — basic version with 160hp (119.3kW) Lycoming IO-320-
  D2A engine. Available as two-seat aerobatic, three-seat utility or four-
  seat version; **FA200-180** — with 180hp
  (134.2kW) Lycoming, also in
  two/three/four-seat versions; **FA200-
  180AO** — with fixed-pitch propeller
  and standard non-injected Lycoming
  O-360-A5AD engine as a low-cost
  equivalent.

**Right and below:**
**Fuji FA200-160 Aero Subaru.** *DJM*

## Grob G-109 Ranger
Two-seat side-by-side motor glider
Basic data for Grob G-109B
*Powerplant:* One 90hp (67kW) GVW 2500 engine
*Span:* 57ft 2in (17.43m)
*Length:* 26ft 7in (8.08m)
*Max cruising speed:* 118mph (190km/h)
*Accommodation:* Two side-by-side seats
*First aircraft flown:* 14 March 1980 (G109); 18 March 1983 (G-109B)
*Production:* G-109 — 151; G-109B — 377
*Recognition:* High-aspect ratio wing. Glass reinforced plastic (GRP) construction
    with fixed tailwheel undercarriage and T-tail.
*Variants:* **G-109** — original model with upward-hinged canopy and 90hp
    (74.6kW) Limbach L200-E1 engine and folding wings; **G-109B** — has longer-
    span wings, larger sliding canopy with fixed wing; **Vigilant T1** — version of
    G-109B for RAF Air Cadets (53 supplied).

***Above and left:***
**Grob G-109B Ranger.** *PRM*

## Grob G-115 Heron
Single-engined two-seat all-plastic light aircraft
Basic data for Grob G-115A
*Powerplant:* One 116hp (88kW) Lycoming O-235-H2C piston engine
*Span:* 34ft 9in (10.60m)
*Length:* 22ft 8in (6.90m)
*Max cruising speed:* 127mph (205km/h)
*Accommodation:* Two side-by-side seats
*First aircraft flown:* 15 November 1985 (G-115); 28 April 1988 (G-115B)
*Production:* 143
*Recognition:* Single-engined low-wing monoplane with fixed undercarriage
and wheel spats. Very smooth lines and finish as built of GRP. Straight
leading edge to wing and tapering trailing edge. Sliding domed fully glazed
canopy. Swept fin and rudder with tailplane set on fuselage.
*Variants:* **G-115** — developed from G-112 with longer fuselage and sliding
canopy, main production version; **G-115B** — with 160hp (119.3kW)
Lycoming 0-320 engine; **G-115C** — with increased capacity fuel tanks in
wings, improved two-piece canopy and rear cockpit luggage area. **G-115D** —
with 180hp (134.2kW) Lycoming AEIO-360-B engine and stressed for
aerobatics. Named Bavarian for US market and Heron in service with the
Airwork-operated RN Flying Grading Flight. **G-115T** — stressed for
aerobatics, fitted with retractable tricycle undercarriage and 260hp
(193.9kW) Lycoming AEIO-540D4A5 engine and four-blade constant speed
propeller. **G-116** — four-seat G-115 with 200hp (149.1kW) Lycoming IO-360-
A, first flown 29 April 1988. **G-115T Acro** is an aerobatic version with a
retractable undercarriage.

**Grob G-115T Acro.** *PRM*

# Grumman American/American Aviation AA-1 Yankee

Single-engined two-seat light aircraft
Basic data for Grumman-American AA-1B Trainer
*Powerplant:* One 108hp (80.5kW) Lycoming O-235-C2C piston engine
*Span:* 24ft 6in (7.47m)
*Length:* 19ft 3in (5.86m)
*Max cruising speed:* 124mph (200km/h)
*Accommodation:* Pilot plus passenger/student
*First aircraft flown:* 1963 (Yankee); 25 March 1970 (AA-1B)
*Production:* Yankee — 461; Trainer — 1,150

*Recognition:* Single-engined low-wing monoplane. Wing of parallel chord with
  square tips. Unusual tubular nosewheel strut angled in front of wheel. Low-
  set angular tailplane. Pointed fin and rudder. Small angular window on each
  side behind main canopy.

*Variants:* **AA-1 Yankee** — basic two-seat model developed from Bede BD-1;
  **AA-1A Trainer** — dual-control trainer version; **AA-1B Trainer** —
  development by Grumman; **AA-1C** —
  more powerful engine. Built by
  Gulfstream American Corporation;
  **AA-1C T-Cat/Lynx** — AA-1 fitted
  with AA-5 tailplane and 115hp
  (85.8kW) Lycoming 0-235-L2C engine.

*Above and right:*
**Grumman American AA-1ATrainer.**
**BSS**

37

# Grumman-American AA-5 Traveler/Cheetah/Tiger

Single-engined four-seat light aircraft
Basic data for Grumman-American AA-5A Cheetah
*Powerplant:* One 150hp (112kW) Lycoming O-320-E2G piston engine
*Span:* 31ft 6in (9.60m)
*Length:* 22ft 0in (6.71m)
*Max cruising speed:* 147mph (237km/h)
*Accommodation:* Pilot plus three passengers
*First aircraft flown:* 21 August 1970
*Production:* AA-5 Traveler — 831; AA-5A Cheetah — 900; AA-5B/AG-5B
Tiger — 1492
*Recognition:* Low-wing monoplane with fixed spatted tricycle undercarriage.
Upright single fin and rudder with pronounced dorsal fillet forward of fin.
Wings of parallel chord with square tips and small fillets at wing roots, both
forward and rear. Oblong tailplane.
*Variants:* **AA-5 Traveler** — original version developed from AA-1 series;
**AA-5A Cheetah** — larger fin fillet, longer rear window; **AA-5B Tiger** —
with 180hp (134.2kW) Lycoming O-360-4AK.

*Above:* Grumman American AA-5A
Cheetah. *DJM*

*Right:* Grumman American AA-5
Traveler. *PRM*

# Grumman (Gulfstream/American) GA-7 Cougar

Twin-engined three/five-seat light business aircraft
Basic data for GA-7 Cougar
*Powerplant:* Two 160hp (119kW) Lycoming O-320-D1D piston engines
*Span:* 36ft 10in (11.23m)
*Length:* 29ft 10in (9.10m)
*Max cruising speed:* 184mph (296km/h)
*Accommodation:* Pilot plus three/five passengers
*First aircraft flown:* 20 December 1974
*Production:* 115
*Recognition:* Twin-engined low-wing monoplane. Retractable tricycle
   undercarriage. Wings of parallel chord and square tips. Cabin entry door.
   Three windows each side. Pointed nose. Swept fin and rudder.
*Variants:* Now built in France by SOCATA as **TB-360 Tangara.**

*Above:* **Grumman
American/Gulfstream GA-7 Cougar.**
*PRM*

*Left:* **SOCATA Tangara.** *PRM*

## HOAC Austria DV.20 Katana

Single-engined two-seat light aircraft
Basic data for HOAC DV.20 Katana
*Powerplant:* One 80hp (59.6kW) Rotax 912A.3 piston engine
*Span:* 35ft 5in (10.8m); 7ft 1in (2.16m) with wings folded
*Length:* 23ft 3.5in (7.1m)
*Max cruising speed:* 140mph (225km/h)
*Accommodation:* Two, side-by-side
*First aircraft flown:* 17 December 1991
*Production:* Over 180 delivered by late 1996. In addition to production in
   Austria a second production line has been set up as Dimona Aircraft in
   London, Ontario, building 17 per month.
*Recognition:* A lightweight short-wing derivative of the Austrian Hoffman H-36
   Dimona. A wholly glass-fibre aircraft with side-by-side dual seating, a T-tail
   and a fixed glass-fibre tricycle undercarriage. Humped canopy slopes
   to a thin tubular rear fuselage. Single-piece side-hinged canopy.
   Wings of constant taper and upturned tips.
*Variants:* **HOAC DV/40** — a development for a four-seat version.

**HOAC Austria DV.20 Katana.** *PRM*

## Jodel D.9/D.11 series

**SAN Jodel D.117.** *PRM*

Single-engined ultra-light aircraft
Basic data for Jodel Wassmer D.120 Paris-Nice
*Powerplant:* One 90hp (67kW) Continental C90-14F piston engine
*Span:* 26ft 11in (8.22m)
*Length:* 21ft 4in (6.50m)
*Max cruising speed:* 121mph (195km/h)
*Accommodation:* Two side-by-side seats
*First aircraft flown:* 21 January 1948 (D.9); 5 May 1950 (D.11)
*Production:* Factory-built — 1,584 (plus many amateur-built versions)
*Recognition:* Single-engined low-wing monoplane with cranked wing. Fixed
  taildragger configuration undercarriage. Sometimes with wheel spats.
*Variants:* **D.9** Bebe — 25hp (18.7kW) Poinsard engine; **D.11** — 45hp (33.6kW)
  Salmson 9Adb engine; **D.111** — pre-production versions with 75hp (55.9kW)
  Minie 4DC engine; **D.112** — factory-built two-seat version of Jodel D.9 with
  65hp (48.5kW) Continental A-65; **D.113** — amateur version of D.112 with
  100hp (74.6kW) Continental O-200-A; **D.114** — amateur version of D.11 with
  70hp (52.2kW) Minie 4DA28; **D.115** — amateur version of D.11 with 75hp
  (55.9kW) Mathis 4-GF-60; **D.116** — amateur version of D.11 with 60hp
  (44.7kW) Salmson 9ADR; **D.117** — SAN/Aepavia built with 90hp (67.1kW)
  Continental C-90; **D.118** — amateur version of D.11 with 60hp (44.7kW)
  Walter Mikron II; **D.119** — amateur version of D.117; **D.120** — Wassmer
  version of D.117 named Paris-Nice; **D.121** — amateur version with 75hp
  (55.9kW) Continental A-75; **D.122** — amateur version with 75hp (55.9kW)
  Praga; **D.123** — amateur version with 85hp (63.4kW) Salmson 5AP01; **D.124**
  — amateur version with 80hp (59.6kW) Salmson 5AQ01; **D.125** — amateur
  version with 90hp (67.1kW) Kaiser; **D.126** — amateur version with 85hp
  (63.4kW) Continental C-85.

# Jodel DR.100 Ambassadeur/Sicile series

Single-engined three/four-seat light aircraft
Basic data for Jodel DR.1050 Ambassadeur
*Powerplant:* One 100hp (74.5kW) Continental O-200-A piston engine
*Span:* 28ft 7in (8.72m)
*Length:* 20ft 10in (6.35m)
*Max cruising speed:* 133mph (215km/h)
*Accommodation:* Normally pilot plus two passengers
*First aircraft flown:* 14 July 1958
*Production:* 810
*Recognition:* Single-engined monoplane with cranked wing and tapered square
   tips. Fixed taildragger undercarriage with wheel spats. Two windows each
   side. Square-tipped fin and rudder.
*Variants:* **DR.100A** — SAN/CEA original version with 90hp (67.1kW) Continental
   C-90; **DR.105A** — SAN/CEA Ambassadeur development; **DR.1050
   Ambassadeur** and **DR.1051 Sicile** — main production versions with
   optional 105hp (78.3kW) Potez 4E-20 engine; **DR.1050M** and **DR.1051M
   Excellence** — sweptback fin and rudder and one-piece elevator;
   **DR.1050MM1 and DR.1051MM1** — Sicile Record. Modifications of DR.1050
   and DR.1051 with sweptback fin and rudder; **D.150 Mascaret** — SAN two-
   seat development of D.117 with
   DR.100 wing and 100hp (74.6kW)
   R-R/Continental O-200-A.

*Right:* **Jodel DR.1050 Ambassadeur.**
*PRM*

*Below:* **CEA DR.1050/M1 Sicile
Record.** *DJM*

# Lake LA-4 Buccaneer/Renegade/Skimmer

Single-engined four-seat amphibian
Basic data for Lake LA-4-200 Buccaneer
*Powerplant:* One 200hp (149kW) Lycoming O-360-A1B piston engine
*Span:* 38ft 0in (11.58m)
*Length:* 24ft 11in (7.59m)
*Max cruising speed:* 150mph (241km/h)
*Accommodation:* Pilot plus four passengers
*First aircraft flown:* November 1959 (Buccaneer); 1982 (Renegade);
  17 July 1948 (Skimmer)
*Production:* Over 1,300 delivered of all versions
*Recognition:* Single-engined shoulder-wing monoplane. Seaplane hull, with
  single step. Long pointed nose. Wheels retract into wings. Fixed wing-tip
  floats. Tractor engine on pylon above cabin. Glazed cabin ahead of leading
  edge of wing. Tall angular fin with tailplane set halfway up fin.
*Variants:* The **Colonial C-1 Skimmer** was the original three-seat
  version that first flew on 17 July 1948. The **C-2 Skimmer** flew in 1957. The
  six-seat **LA-250 Renegade** has a larger cabin, a 250hp (335kW) Lycoming IO-
  540-C4B5 engine, swept vertical tail and first flew in 1982. The **Seawolf** is
  a military version. **Sea Fury** and **Turbo Sea Fury**
  are versions for salt water
  operations. **Lean Machine** is a
  reduced-cost version of the
  Renegade, mainly for
  corporate users.

***Above and right:*** **Lake LA-4
Renegade. *PRM***

# Luscombe Silvaire

All-metal two-seat light aircraft
Basic data for Luscombe Silvaire Deluxe Model 8E
*Powerplant:* One 85hp (63.4kW) Continental C-85 piston engine
*Span:* 35ft 0in (10.66m)
*Length:* 20ft 0in (6.09m)
*Max cruising speed:* 112mph (180km/h)
*Accommodation:* Pilot plus one passenger
*First aircraft flown:* 18 December 1937 (Luscombe); 9 October 1956 (Silvaire)
*Production:* 1938-42 — 1,125; 1945-51 — 4,668
*Recognition:* High-wing metal aircraft with twin V-wing struts. Taildragger
  configuration. Slender rear fuselage.
*Variants:* **Model 8** — original version with 50hp (37.3kW) Continental A-50
  engine; **Model 8A** — known as **Luscombe Master** with 65hp (48.5kW)
  Continental A-65; **Model 8B** — known as **Luscombe Trainer** — with 65hp
  (48.5kW) Lycoming O-145-B; **Model 8C** — Silvaire Deluxe with 75hp (55.9kW)
  Continental A-75; **Model 8D** — Silvaire Deluxe Trainer; **Model 8F** — an 8E
  with 90hp (67.1kW) Continental
  C-90; **Model T8F-Luscombe
  Observer** — tandem two-seat
  version of Model 8F for
  observation duties.

*Right:* **Luscombe 8AE
Silvaire.** *PRM*

*Below:* **Luscombe 8E
Silvaire.** *PRM*

# Mooney M.20-201/231

**Mooney M.20J.** *PRM*

Single-engined four-seat light aircraft
Basic data for Mooney (M.20K) 231
*Powerplant:* One 210hp (156kW) Continental TSIO-360-GB
   turbocharged piston engine
*Span:* 36ft 1in (11.00m)
*Length:* 25ft 5in (7.75m)
*Max cruising speed:* 210mph (338km/h)
*Accommodation:* Pilot plus three passengers
*First aircraft flown:* 10 August 1953 (M.20); June 1976 (201); October 1976 (231)
*Production:* Mooney M.20 — 7,592+; Production continuing
*Recognition:* Single-engined low-wing all-metal monoplane with retractable
   tricycle undercarriage. Recognisable by vertical leading edge to fin and
   rudder. Straight leading edge to wings and tailplane. Pronounced fillet at
   front wing roots.
*Variants:* **M.20** — initial metal/wood version with 150hp (111.9kW) O-320
   engine; **M.20B/C-Mark 21** — all-metal, new windscreen; **M.20E-Super 21** —
   With 200hp (149.1kW) Lycoming engine and refinements. Also named
   Aerostar 201 and Chaparral following purchase of Mooney by Butler
   Aviation; **M.20F Executive/Aerostar 201** — stretched (10in) cabin, three
   side windows and 200hp (149.1kW) Lycoming IO-360-A3B6D; **M.20J/Mooney
   201/205** — modified nose, windscreen and two longer cabin windows;
   **M.20K/Mooney 231/252** — 201 with 210hp (156.6kW) turbocharged
   Continental engine; **Mooney TLS** — formerly M20M introduced 1989 with
   270hp (201.3kW) turbocharged Textron Lycoming TIO-540-AF1A. **Mooney
   Ovation** (M.20R) — first flew May 1994, combines the TLS airframe and
   interior with a 208hp (155.1kW) Teledyne Continental IO-550-G5B engine.

## Morane-Saulnier/SOCATA MS880 Rallye

Single-engined two/four-seat light aircraft
Basic data for MS880B Rallye Club
*Powerplant:* One 100hp (74.5kW) Continental O-200-A piston engine
*Span:* 31ft 11in (9.74m)
*Length:* 23ft 9in (7.24m)
*Max cruising speed:* 119mph (192km/h)
*Accommodation:* Pilot plus two/three passengers
*First aircraft flown:* 10 June 1959 (MS880); 24 May 1961 (MS880B)
*Production:* 1,102
*Recognition:* Metal low-wing monoplane with fixed tricycle undercarriage, large sliding cockpit canopy. Parallel chord wings with rounded tips and noticeable dihedral. Swept fin and rudder with small dorsal fillet. Oblong tailplane set at base of rudder. Deep cabin sides tapering towards tail unit.
*Variants:* **MS880B Rallye Club** — main production version; **MS881 Rallye 105** — with 105hp (78.3kW) Potez 4E-20A engine; **Rallye 100S Sport** — two-seat spinnable trainer version with larger tail; **Rallye 100ST** — two/four-seater 100S with increased take-off weight; **Rallye 100ST Galopin** — Rallye 100ST with 155hp (115.6kW) Lycoming O-320-L2A; **Rallye 150ST** — stressed for spinning; **Rallye 180T Galerien** — with 180hp (134.2kW) Lycoming O-360-A3A engine; **MS883 Rallye 115** — MS880B with large dorsal fin and 115hp (85.7kW) Lycoming O-235-C2A; **MS885 Super Rallye** — MS880B with 145hp (108.1kW) Continental O-300-A.

**SOCATA MS880B Rallye Club.** *PRM*

## Neico Lancair

Single-engined two-seat sporting and cross-country homebuilt aircraft
Basic data for Lancair 320 Mk II
*Powerplant:* One 160hp (119kW) Textron Lycoming O-320 or 180hp (134kW) IO-360 piston engine
*Span:* 23ft 6in (7.16m)
*Length:* 21ft 0in (6.40m)
*Max cruising speed:* 240mph (386km/h)
*Accommodation:* Two, side-by-side
*First aircraft flown:* June 1984 (Lancair 200)
*Production:* Kits have been sold in 34 countries

*Top:* **Neico Lancair 320.** *PRM*

*Above:* **Neico Lancair 235.** *PRM*

*Recognition:* Single-engined low-wing monoplane. Composite airframe of glass fibre, giving very clean lines. Retractable tricycle undercarriage. Swept fin and rudder with square tip. Tailplane set two-thirds up the fin. Large single-piece canopy.

*Variants:* **Lancair 235** — the first model offered in kit form, with 118hp (88kW) O-235 engine; **Lancair 360** — similar to the 320 with 180hp (134kW) Textron Lycoming O-360 engine; **Lancair IV** — introduced in 1990, has conventional seating for four persons and offers extremely high cruising speeds. Fitted with 350hp (261kW) Teledyne Continental TSIO-550-B1B twin-turbocharged twin-intercooled engine; **Lancair ES** — a joint venture between Lancair and a Malaysian organisation;. **Lancair ESP** — a production-assembled version with a 200hp (149kW) Teledyne Continental IO-360-ES and has a retractable undercarriage.

## Partenavia P68 Victor

*Above and below:* Partenavia P68B Victor. *PRM/DJM*

Twin-engined six/seven-seat light transport
Basic data for Partenavia P68C

*Powerplant:* Two 200hp (149kW) Lycoming IO-360-A1B6 piston engines
*Span:* 39ft 4in (12.0m)
*Length:* 31ft 4in (9.55m)
*Max cruising speed:* 191mph (307km/h)
*Accommodation:* Pilot plus up to six passengers
*First aircraft flown:* 25 May 1970
*Production:* 400+
*Recognition:* High-wing monoplane with underslung engines. Sleek fuselage and streamlined nose. Swept fin and rudder with small dorsal fillet. Low-set oblong tailplane with fillet at forward base. Three large cabin windows on each side. Fixed tricycle undercarriage with spats.
*Variants:* **P68** — original version; **P68B** — P68 with 6in fuselage stretch, standard six-seat interior; **P68 Observer** — P68B with fully glazed nose section; **P68C** — P68B with longer nose; **P68C-TC** — with 210hp (156.6kW) Lycoming TO-360-C1A6D turbocharged engines; **P68 TP-300 Spartacus** — P68T with fixed undercarriage, redesigned tailplane and upturned wing tips; **AP68TP-300 Viator** — lengthened fuselage and 11 seats and 330hp (246kW) Allison 250-B17C turboprops, redesigned tailplane and upturned wingtips.

## Piel CP301 Emeraude

Single-engined two-seat light aircraft
Basic data for Piel CP301A Emeraude
*Powerplant:* One 90hp (67kW)
    Continental C90-12F piston engine
*Span:* 26ft 4in (8.04m)
*Length:* 20ft 8in (6.30m)
*Max cruising speed:* 124mph (200km/h)
*Accommodation:* Two side-by-side
*First aircraft flown:* 19 June 1954
*Production:* 251

*Recognition:* Low-wing monoplane with elliptical wingtips. Short nose, domed
    one-piece cockpit canopy. Taildragger undercarriage, sometimes with
    mainwheel spats. Rounded fin and rudder.

*Variants:* **CP301A** — commercial production model; **CP301B** — with smaller
    control surfaces and sliding cockpit cover and spatted undercarriage, built by
    Rousseau; **CP301C** — taller bubble canopy, pointed wingtips, modified tail
    and new engine cowling, built by Scintex; **CP301S Smaragd** — German-built
    version by Schempp Hirth for Binder Aviatik; **CP320** — powered by 100hp
    (74.6kW) Continental O-200-A. The CAP10 was developed from the
    Emeraude. **CP328 Super Emeraude** developed from the Emeraude with a
    100-115 hp (74.6-87.5kW) Teledyne Continental engine.

*Top:* **Scintex CP301-C3 Super Emeraude.** *PRM*

*Above* **right: Scintex CP301-C2 Emeraude.** *PRM*

## Piper J/3C Cub/PA-18 Super Cub

Single-engined tandem two-seat high-wing light aircraft
Basic data for PA-18-150 Super Cub
*Powerplant:* One 150hp (112kW) Lycoming O-320 piston engine
*Span:* 35ft 4in (10.76m)
*Length:* 22ft 7in (6.88m)
*Max cruising speed:* 115mph (185km/h)
*Accommodation:* Two tandem seats
*First aircraft flown:* 1938
*Production:* Civil — 14,124; Military (L-4) — 5,673
*Recognition:* High-wing tube and fabric monoplane. Twin V-struts to wings.
   Equal chord wings with rounded tips. Braced fixed taildragger undercarriage
   with cross bracings between wheels. Pointed fin and rudder. Elliptical
   tailplane. Earlier models have uncowled cylinder heads.
*Variants:* **J/3 Cub** — original version with uncowled cylinder heads;
   Continental, Lycoming or Franklin engine of various horsepower ratings
   between 50 and 100 (37.3-74.6kW); **J/3C-65 Cub Special/PA-11 Cub Special**
   — postwar versions with 65hp (48.5kW) Continental A-65 engine; **PA-18
   Super Cub** — Introduced in 1952 with Continental C-90; last production
   version featured a 150hp (111.9kW) Lycoming O-320 piston engine; **Piper
   PA-18-150 Super Cub** — production resumed in 1988.

*Above:* Piper J/3C-85 Cub. *PRM*

*Right:* Piper PA-18-95 Super Cub.
*BSS*

## Piper PA-20 Pacer/PA-22 Colt and Tri-Pacer

Single-engined four-seat light aircraft
Basic data for Piper PA-20-135 Pacer
*Powerplant:* One 135hp (101kW) Lycoming O-290-D2 piston engine
*Span:* 29ft 4in (8.94m)
*Length:* 20ft 5in (6.22m)
*Max cruising speed:* 112mph (180km/h)
*Accommodation:* Pilot plus three passengers
*First aircraft flown:* July 1949
*Production:* PA-20 Pacer — 1,120; PA-22 Tri-Pacer/Colt — 9,490
*Recognition:* High-wing monoplane with V-struts to wing from top of
   undercarriage legs. Twin glazed windows on each side. Fully cowled engine.
   Cantilever undercarriage legs with wheel spats. PA-20 has taildragger
   configuration. PA-22 has a tricycle undercarriage. Rounded fin and rudder.
   Mid-position tailplane with wire bracing.
*Variants:* **PA-20 Pacer** — original version developed from PA-16 Clipper; **PA-22
   Tri-Pacer** — PA-20 with fixed tricycle undercarriage and 125hp (93.2kW)
   Lycoming O-290-D engine; **PA-22-108 Colt** — two-seat trainer version of Tri-
   Pacer without rear side windows. 108hp (80.5kW) Lycoming O-235-C1 engine;
   **PA-22-160** — with 160hp (119.3kW) Lycoming O-320-B; **Caribbean** —
   low-cost version of Tri-Pacer, introduced 1958.

*Top:* Piper PA-22-108 Tailwheel Colt. *PRM*

*Above right:* Piper PA-22-108 Colt. *PRM*

## Piper PA-23 Apache/Aztec

Twin-engined four/six-seat light business aircraft
Basic data for Piper PA-23-250 Aztec E
*Powerplant:* Two 250hp (186kW) Lycoming IO-540-C4B5 piston engines
*Span:* 37ft 4in (11.37m)
*Length:* 31ft 3in (9.52m)
*Accommodation:* Pilot plus three/five passengers
*Max cruising speed:* 206mph (332km/h)
*First aircraft flown:* 2 March 1952
*Production:* PA-23 Apache — 2,165; PA-23 Aztec — 4,811
*Recognition:* Twin-engined low-wing monoplane. Retractable tricycle
  undercarriage. Wings of equal chord with rounded tips. Pronounced fillet at
  front wing roots. Three glazed windows on each side. Apache has a short
  nose, curved fin, rudder and tailplane. Aztec has a more bulbous cabin, a
  larger square-cut slightly swept fin and rudder and square-cut tailplane.
*Variants:* **PA-23 Apache** — light twin developed from the Twin Stinson; **PA-
  23-250 Aztec B** — with longer nose incorporating baggage compartment,
  six-seat interior; **PA-23-250 Aztec C/D/E/F** — improved versions with
  optional turbocharged engines.

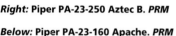

*Right:* **Piper PA-23-250 Aztec B.** *PRM*

*Below:* **Piper PA-23-160 Apache.** *PRM*

## Piper PA-24 Comanche
Single-engined four-seat cabin monoplane
Basic data for Piper PA-24-260 Comanche C
*Powerplant:* One 260hp (194kW) Lycoming IO-540-E piston engine
*Span:* 36ft 0in (10.97m)
*Length:* 25ft 0in (7.62m)
*Accommodation:* Pilot plus three passengers
*Max cruising speed:* 185mph (298km/h)
*First aircraft flown:* 24 May 1956
*Production:* 4,716
*Recognition:* Low-wing cabin monoplane with retractable undercarriage. Two
   cabin windows on each side. Swept fin and rudder with low-set tailplane at
   fuselage extremity.
*Variants:* **PA-24-180** — original version with 180hp (134.2kW) Lycoming O-360-
   A1A engine; **PA-24-250/260/300/380** — differing engine sizes; **PA-24-400** —
   final version with 400hp (298.3kW) Lycoming IGSO-720-A1A engine and
   three-blade propeller.

*Above:* **Piper PA-24-260 Comanche D.**
*PRM*

*Left:* **Piper PA-24-250 Comanche.** *PRM*

# Piper PA-25 Pawnee/36 Pawnee Brave

Single-engined single-seat agricultural aircraft
Basic data for Piper PA-25-235 Pawnee D
*Powerplant:* One 260hp (193.9kW) Lycoming O-540-G1A5 piston engine
*Span:* 36ft 2in (11.02m)
*Length:* 24ft 8in (7.53m)
*Max cruising speed:* 114mph (183km/h)
*Accommodation:* Single-seat
*First aircraft flown:* 1957 (PA-25); 5 December 1969 (PA-36)
*Production:* PA-25 — 5,169; PA-36 — 938
*Recognition:* Single-engined low-wing single-seat strut-braced agricultural
  aircraft. Fixed tailwheel undercarriage. Raised glazed cockpit canopy. Parallel
  chord wings with rounded tips. Spray system attached to underneath trailing
  edge of wings. Square-topped fin and rudder on PA-36.
*Variants:* **PA-25-150** — initial version with 150hp (111.9kW) O-320 engine;
  **PA-25-235** — with 235hp (175.2kW) O-540-B2B5 engine; **Pawnee B** —
  improved PA-25-235 with larger hopper; **Pawnee C** — with 260hp (193.9kW)
  O-540-E engine; **PA-36 Pawnee Brave** — originally known as Pawnee II.
  Larger than PA-25 with cantilever wings and swept-back fin and rudder.
  Fitted with either 300hp (223.7kW) Lycoming IO-540-K1G5 or 375hp
  (279.6kW) Lycoming IO-720-D1CD.

*Above and right:* **Piper PA-25-260 Pawnee D.** *DJM/PRM*

**Piper PA-28-161 Cherokee Warrior II.** *PRM*

# Piper PA-28 Cherokee series

Single-engined four-seat light aircraft
Basic data for Piper PA-28-181 Archer II
*Powerplant:* One 180hp (134kW) Lycoming O-360-A4M piston engine
*Span:* 35ft 0in (10.67m)
*Length:* 23ft 9in (7.26m)
*Max cruising speed:* 148mph (239km/h)
*Accommodation:* Pilot plus three passengers
*First aircraft flown:* 10 January 1960 (Cherokee); 27 August 1976 (Warrior II)
*Production:* 29,285+
*Recognition:* Low-wing monoplane. Wings, with pronounced dihedral, of equal
    chord with rounded tips. Outer wings on later models were tapered. Fillet at
    front wing root. Fixed tricycle undercarriage, with mainwheel spats. Swept
    fin and rudder with dorsal fillet. Low-set oblong tailplane. Trim options
    included Standard, Custom, Super Custom.
*Variants:* **PA-28-140/150/160/180 Cherokee B-F** — with different powered
    engines; **PA-28-140 Cruiser** — touring version of 140 trainer; **PA-28-151
    Warrior** — with new wing incorporating tapering outer panels; **PA-28-161
    Warrior II** — Lycoming O-320-D2G; **-161 Cadet** — basic 2+2 trainer; **PA-28-
    180 Challenger/Archer** — with 5in fuselage stretch, 2ft wingspan increase,
    longer cabin and redesigned tail; **PA-28-181 Archer II** — new wing with
    tapering outer panels and 180hp (134.2kW) Lycoming; **PA-28-235
    Charger/Pathfinder** — 235hp (175.2kW) Lycoming O-540-B4B5 and larger
    windows; **PA-28-236 Dakota** — Pathfinder with new tapered wing; **PA-28-
    201 Turbo Dakota** — with 200hp (149.1kW) Lycoming TSIO-360-FB.

# Piper PA-28R Cherokee Arrow

Single-engined four-seat touring aircraft
Basic data for Piper PA-28R-180 Arrow
*Powerplant:* One 180hp (134kW) Lycoming IO-360-B1E piston engine
*Span:* 35ft 0in (10.67m)
*Length:* 25ft 0in (7.62m)
*Max cruising speed:* 165mph (266km/h)
*Accommodation:* Pilot plus three passengers
*First aircraft flown:* 1 February 1967
*Production:* 6,797
*Recognition:* As Cherokee 180 with three side windows and retractable
   undercarriage. Low wing of equal chord with rounded tips. Outer wings on
   later models are tapered. Fillet at front wing root. Swept fin and rudder with
   dorsal fillet. Low-set oblong tailplane.
*Variants:* PA-28R-180 initial version; **PA-28R-200** — with 200hp (149.1kW)
   Lycoming IO-360-CIC; **Arrow B** — minor improvements; **PA-28R-200
   Cherokee Arrow II** — longer (5in) fuselage version of Arrow B; **PA-28R-201
   Arrow III** — longer span (3ft) tapered wing; also turbo version; **PA-28RT-
   201 Arrow IV** — new rear fuselage with T-tail; also turbo version.

**Right and below: Piper PA-28R-200
Cherokee Arrow II. *PRM***

## Piper PA-30/39 Twin Comanche
Twin-engined four/six-seater business aircraft
Basic data for Piper PA-39 Twin Comanche C/R
*Powerplant:* Two 160hp (119kW) Lycoming IO-320-B1A piston engines
*Span:* 36ft 9in (11.22m)
*Length:* 25ft 2in (7.67m)
*Max cruising speed:* 198mph (319km/h)
*Accommodation:* Pilot plus three/five passengers
*First aircraft flown:* 7 November 1962
*Production:* PA-30 — 2,001; PA-39 — 155
*Recognition:* Low-wing twin-engined monoplane with retractable tricycle
  undercarriage. Straight leading wing edge with pronounced fillet at front
  wing root. Engines mounted high on leading edge of wing. Swept fin and
  rudder with low-set tapered tailplane. Some models have wingtip fuel tanks.
*Variants:* **PA-30 Twin Comanche B** — third cabin window on each side and
  optional fifth/sixth seats. Optional turbocharged engine; **PA-30 Twin
  Comanche C** — improved IO-320 engines. Optional wing tip tanks; **PA 30
  Twin Comanche C/R** — with contra-rotating propellers to eliminate torque
  effects — became known as PA-39 from 1971; also turbocharged option with
  TIO-320-C1A engines.

*Above:* **Piper PA-30-160 Twin
Comanche C.** *PRM*

*Right:* **Piper PA-30-160 Twin
Comanche B.** *DJM*

# Piper PA-32 Cherokee Six/Saratoga/Lance

Single-engined six/seven-seat light aircraft
Basic data for Piper PA-32-301 Saratoga
*Powerplant:* One 300hp (224kW) Lycoming IO-540-K1G5 piston engine
*Span:* 36ft 2in (11.02m)
*Length:* 27ft 8in (8.44m)
*Max cruising speed:* 175mph (282km/h)
*Accommodation:* Pilot plus five/six passengers
*First aircraft flown:* 6 December 1963
*Production:* PA-32 Cherokee Six/Saratoga — 4,432; PA-32 Cherokee Lance — 2,808
*Recognition:* Cherokee Six: large single-engine low-wing monoplane. Equal chord wing with rounded tips. Four windows on each side. Fixed tricycle undercarriage with wheel spats. Saratoga has retractable undercarriage with semi-tapered wing. Lance has T-tail. Turbocharged version has large air inlet beneath the propeller spinner.
*Variants:* **PA-32-260 Cherokee Six** — PA-28 with 30in rear fuselage stretch and forward baggage compartment., six seats with optional seventh; **PA-32-300 Cherokee Six** — with 300hp (223.7kW) Lycoming IO-540-K; **PA-32-301 Saratoga** — PA-32-300 with wing based on that of PA-28-151 Warrior; **PA-32-301T Saratoga** — turbocharged version with new nose line; **PA-32R-300 Cherokee Lance** — Retractable undercarriage version of Cherokee Six known just as 'Lance' from 1977; **PA-32R-300 Lance II** — new T-tail; also turbocharged version; **PA-32R-301 Saratoga SP** — retractable undercarriage version, with standard tail; also turbocharged version; **PA-32R-301 Saratoga II HP** — Saratoga SP with reduced-depth side windows.

**Piper PA-32-300 Cherokee Six B.** *PRM*

# Piper PA-34 Seneca

Twin-engined six-passenger light transport and trainer
Basic data for Piper PA-34 Seneca II
*Powerplant:* Two 200hp (149kW) Continental TSIO-360-E piston engines
*Span:* 38ft 11in (11.85m)
*Length:* 28ft 7in (8.73m)
*Max cruising speed:* 219mph (285km/h)
*Accommodation:* Pilot plus five passengers
*First aircraft flown:* 30 August 1968
*Production:* 4,560
*Recognition:* Twin-engine low-wing monoplane. Engines set high on leading
   edge of wings. Long pointed nose. Tapering fuselage. Four cabin windows
   each side. Wings of parallel chord with rounded tips and fillet at front wing
   root. Swept fin and rudder. Low-mounted oblong tailplane.
*Variants:* **PA-34-200 Seneca** — original model with two 180hp (134.2kW)
   Lycoming O-360 piston engines; **PA-34-200T Seneca II** — turbocharged
   Seneca, optional club seating, seventh seat; **PA-34-220T Seneca III** — with
   two turbocharged 220hp (164.0kW) Continental TSIO-360-KB2A engines and
   single-piece windscreen; **PA-34-220T Seneca IV** — Seneca III
   with reduced-depth side windows,
   new engine cowlings and
   upgraded interior.

*Above:* **Piper PA-34-200T Seneca II.**
**PRM**

*Right:* **Piper PA-34-220T Seneca III.**
**PRM**

# Piper PA-38-112 Tomahawk

Single-engined two-seat aerobatic trainer
Basic data for Piper PA-38-112 Tomahawk
*Powerplant:* One 112hp (83.5kW) Lycoming O-235-L2C piston engine
*Span:* 34ft 0in (10.36m)
*Length:* 23ft 2in (7.04m)
*Max cruising speed:* 126mph (202km/h)
*Accommodation:* Two side-by-side seats
*First aircraft flown:* 1977
*Production:* 2,519
*Recognition:* Low-wing monoplane with fixed tricycle undercarriage. Tailplane mounted high on the fin. No rear fuselage decking behind cabin which has 360° visibility. Wing of equal chord and rounded tips. Oblong tailplane with small cut-out at fin.
*Variants:* None

***Above and right:*** **Piper PA-38-112 Tomahawk.** *PRM*

# Piper PA-44 Seminole

Twin-engined lightweight four-seat aircraft
Basic data for Piper PA-44-180 Seminole
*Powerplant:* One each 180hp (134kW) Lycoming O-360-E1A6D and one LO-360-
E1A6D contra-rotating piston engines
*Span:* 38ft 7in (11.77m)
*Length:* 27ft 7in (8.41m)
*Max cruising speed:* 192mph (309km/h)
*Accommodation:* Pilot plus three passengers
*First aircraft flown:* May 1976
*Production:* 481
*Recognition:* Twin-engined low-wing monoplane with T-tail. Retractable
tricycle undercarriage. Slightly swept leading edge to wings with blunt tips.
Three windows each side.
*Variants:* **PA-44-180 Seminole** — standard model; **PA-44-180T Seminole** —
with 180hp (134.2kW) TO-360-E1AD/LTO-360-E1A6D turbocharged engines.

*Above and left:* Piper PA-44-180
Seminole. *DJM/PRM*

# Pitts S-1/S-2

Single-engined sporting and competition aerobatic biplane
Basic data for Pitts S-2A
*Powerplant:* One 200hp (149kW) Lycoming AEIO-360-A1A piston engine
*Span:* 20ft 0in (6.10m)
*Length:* 17ft 9in (5.79m)
*Max cruising speed:* 152mph (245km/h)
*Accommodation:* One or two seats
*First aircraft flown:* 1943; no longer supplied in kit form
*Production:* 598 (factory produced versions). Also many amateur-built S-1/S-2s
*Recognition:* Small biplane with slightly swept upper wing and straight edged
   lower wing of unequal length. Rounded wingtips. Fixed tailwheel
   undercarriage with spats to main wheel. Dorsal fairing behind cockpit.
   Rounded fin and rudder with elliptical tailplane. Numerous bracing wires.
*Variants:* **S-1 Special** — original factory-built single-seat version with ailerons
   on lower wings only; **S-1C/D/E** — amateur-built versions; **S-1S/T** — factory
   built for competition aerobatics; S-1T also available in kit form; **S-2A** —
   scaled-up S-1 with tandem two-seat
fuselage; **S-2B** — with 260hp
(193.9kW) Lycoming AEIO-540-D4A5
engine, upper wings moved forward
6in; **S-2S** — without front cockpit and
with twin-tank fuel system; **S-2SE** —
amateur-built S-2S from factory-
produced kit.

***Right and below:*** **Pitts S-1C Special.
PRM**

# Robin DR220/250/300 series

Single-engined two/four-seat light aircraft

Basic data for CEA/Robin DR221 Dauphin

*Powerplant:* One 108hp (80.5kW) Rolls-Royce/Continental O-235-C2A piston engine

*Span:* 28ft 7in (8.72m)

*Length:* 22ft 11in (7.0m)

*Max cruising speed:* 127mph (205km/h)

*Accommodation:* Pilot plus one/three passengers

*First aircraft flown:* 5 February 1966

*Production:* DR220 2+2 — 83; DR221 Dauphin — 62; DR253 — 100; DR315 — 388+

**Top: Robin DR315 Petit Prince.** *PRM*

**Above: Robin DR221 Dauphin.** *PRM*

*Recognition:* Low-wing wooden monoplane with typical 'Jodel' cranked wing. DR221 has 'tail dragger' configuration; DR200 has tricycle undercarriage with wheel spats. Large glazed cockpit.

*Variants:* **DR200** — development of DR1050M with full four-seat cabin; **DR220 2+2** — DR220 with two seats and rear children's seat; **DR221 Dauphin** — DR220 with full four seats and all-flying tailplane; **DR250 Capitaine** — with 160hp (119.3kW) Lycoming O-320-D2A engine and seating for four adults; **DR253 Regent** — tricycle undercarriage, larger fuselage and 180hp (134.2kW) Lycoming O-360-D2A; **DR315 Petit Prince** — DR221 with tricycle undercarriage and 115hp (85.8kW) Lycoming; **DR300-108 2+2** — development of DR315; **DR300-120** — four-seat DR300 with 120hp (89.5kW) Lycoming O-235-L2A; also **DR300-140, -180.**

# Robin DR400 series

Single-engined two/four-seat light aircraft
Basic data for Robin DR400-180 Regent
*Powerplant:* One 180hp (134kW) Lycoming O-320-A piston engine
*Span:* 28ft 7in (8.72m)
*Length:* 22ft 10in (6.96m)
*Max cruising speed:* 133mph (215km/h)
*Accommodation:* Pilot plus three passengers
*First aircraft flown:* 27 March 1972
*Production:* 1,458
*Recognition:* Low-wing monoplane with 'Jodel' cranked wing and square tips.
   Fixed tricycle undercarriage with wheel spats. Oblong mid-set tailplane has
   pronounced trim tabs. Large fairings at front wing roots.
   Forward-sliding canopy.
*Variants:* **DR400-100 Cadet** — two-seat trainer; **DR400-108 Dauphin** — two
   plus two trainer; **DR400-120 Dauphin 2+2** — additional windows; **DR400-
   140 Earl** — forward-sliding canopy; **DR400-160 Chevalier** — with
   Lycoming O-320-D2A; **DR400-180 Regent** — forward-sliding canopy;
   additional windows; **DR400-180
   Regent III** — DR400 'Nouvelle
   Generation'; **DR400-180R
   Remorquer** — glider tug; **DR400-
   200R Remo 200** — DR400 glider tug
   with 200hp (149.1kW) Lycoming IO-
   360-A1-B6 and without extra rear
   side windows.

*Right:* **Robin DR400-140B Major.** *PRM*

*Below:* **Robin DR400-180 Regent.** *PRM*

*Above:* **Robin HR200/120. PRM**

# Robin HR100/200 series

Single-engined two/five-seat light training/touring aircraft
Basic data for Robin HR100-285 Tiara
*Powerplant:* One 285hp (210kW) Continental Tiara 6-285B piston engine
*Span:* 29ft 10in (9.08m)
*Length:* 24ft 11in (7.59m)
*Max cruising speed:* 193mph (310km/h)
*Accommodation:* Pilot plus four passengers
*First aircraft flown:* 18 November 1972 (HR100-285); 3 February 1976 (HR100-180)
*Production:* HR100 series — 243; HR200 series — 214
*Recognition:* Conventional constant-chord low-wing monoplane without the 'Jodel' cranked wing. High back fuselage with slab tailplane at the base of the rectangular fin. Divided front windscreen and single side window. Retractable undercarriage.
*Variants:* **HR100-180** — all metal low-wing of constant chord; **HR100-200B Royal** — with 200hp (149.1kW) Lycoming IO-360-AD engine and **HR100-210 Safari** with 210hp (156.6kW) Continental IO-360-D were the main production versions; **HR100-250TR Tiara** — with 250hp (186.4kW) Tiara engine; **R1180T Aiglon** — sleeker HR100-180 with longer cabin windows; **HR200/100 Club** — smaller, all-metal, two-seat version of HR100 with fixed tricycle undercarriage and 108hp (80.5kW) Lycoming engine; **R2100 Super Club** — aerobatic version of HR200/100 with larger fin and rudder; **R2160 Alpha Sport** — R2100 with 160hp (119.3kW) O-320-D2A engine; **R2160A** — R2160 with full aerobatic equipment.

## Rockwell Commander 112/114

Single-engined four-seat light aircraft
Basic data for Rockwell Commander 114
*Powerplant:* 260hp (194kW) Lycoming IO-540-T4B5D piston engine
*Span:* 35ft 7in (10.85m)
*Length:* 25ft 0in (7.62m)
*Accomodation:* Pilot plus three passengers
*Max cruising speed:* 181mph (291km/h)
*First aircraft flown:* 4 December 1970
*Production:* Commander 112 — 801; Commander 114 — 509
*Recognition:* Low-wing monoplane with retractable tricycle undercarriage.
  Straight leading edge to wing with fairing at front root. Tapered trailing
  edge with square tips. Large swept fin and rudder with dorsal fairing from
  cabin. Very small ventral strake. Twin side windows. Tapered tailplane set
  half-way up the fin.
*Variants:* **112** — original basic model with 200hp (149.1kW) Lycoming IO-360-
  C1D6 engine; **112A** — Structurally strengthened model; **112B** — 34in
  wingspan increase, larger wheels; **112TC** — turbocharged version with
  210hp (156.6kW) Lycoming TIO-360-C1A6D engine; **114** — with 260hp
  (193.9kW) engine; **114A** — gran turismo model; **114B** — with new McCauley
  propeller, smaller air intakes and IO-540-T4B5D engine. **114AT** — advanced
  Trainer, for primary training; **114TC** is a turbocharged version.

*Above:* Rockwell Commander 114.
PRM

*Left:* Rockwell Commander 112B.
PRM

# Rollason (Druine) D.31 Turbulent

Single-seat ultra-light aircraft
Basic data for Rollason (Druine) D.31 Turbulent
*Powerplant:* One 45hp (33.5kW) Rollason-Ardem 4C02 MkIV or 55hp (41.0kW)
 MkV engine (conversion of VW engine)
*Span:* 21ft 7in (6.58m)
*Length:* 17ft 6in (5.33m)
*Max cruising speed:* 100mph (161km/h)
*Accommodation:* Single-seat
*First aircraft flown:* 1951
*Production:* Rollason — 29; Stark — 35; also many homebuilt examples
*Recognition:* Low-wing monoplane with fixed taildragger undercarriage with
 tail skid. Wings of parallel chord with rounded tips. Open cockpit. Small
 upright fin and rudder. Oblong tailplane, set forward of fin, with rounded
 tips. Exposed engine cylinder heads on each side immediately behind spinner.
*Variants:* **D.3** — initial French version; **D.31** — standard Rollason-built version.
 Early aircraft had 30hp (22.3kW) Ardem or Porsche engines; **D.31A** —
 Rollason-developed version with 45hp
 (33.5kW) Ardem MkX engine;
 **Turbulent D** — built by Stark in
 Germany. Fully transparent cockpit
 canopy. 45hp (33.5kW) Stark Stamo
 1400 engine.

***Above and Right:* Rollason/Druine
D.31 Turbulent.** *PRM*

67

## Rollason (Druine) D.62 Condor

Two-seat ultra-light aircraft
Basic data for Rollason D.62B Condor
*Powerplant:* One 100hp (74.5kW) Rolls-Royce Continental O-200-A
    piston engine
*Span:* 27ft 6in (8.38m)
*Length:* 22ft 6in (6.86m)
*Max cruising speed:* 115mph (185km/h)
*Accommodation:* Two side-by-side seats
*First aircraft flown:* 1956 (Druine); May 1961 (Rollason)
*Production:* 51 by Rollason
*Recognition:* Single-engined low-wing monoplane with fixed tailwheel
    undercarriage. Enclosed side-by-side cockpit. Tapered wings and tailplane
    with rounded tips. Upright tailfin and rudder with small dorsal fillet.
    Cowled engine.
*Variants:* **D.62A** — pre-production version; **D.62B** — standard production
    version with flaps; **D.62C** — glider-towing version with 130hp (96.9kW) Rolls-
    Royce Continental O-240-A engine. Raised canopy.

***Right and below:*** **Rollason/Druine
D.62B Condor.** *PRM*

# Rutan Long-Ez/Varieze/Cozy

Two-seat high-performance homebuilt sporting aircraft

Basic data for Rutan Varieze

*Powerplant:* Varieze — One 100hp (74.6kW) Continental 0-200B piston engine
Long-Ez — One 115hp (85.8kW) Avco Lycoming O-235 or 100hp (74.6kW)
Continental O-200B Cozy — One 118hp (88.0kW) Avco Lycoming O-235-L2C

*Span:* Varieze — 22ft 2½in (6.77m); Long-Ez — 26ft 1¼in (7.90m);
Cozy — 20ft 1¼in (7.96m)

*Length:* Varieze — 14ft 2in (4.32m); Long-Ez & Cozy — 16ft 9½in (5.12m)

*Max cruising speed:* Varieze — 195mph (313km/h); Long-Ez — 183mph
(295km/h); Cozy — 180mph (290km/h)

*Accommodation:* Varieze/Long-Ez — Pilot plus one (tandem); Cozy — Pilot plus
one (side-by-side)

*First aircraft flown:* Varieze — 21 May 1975; Long-Ez — 12 June 1979;
Cozy — 19 July 1982

*Production:* All available in kit form or from plans

*Recognition:* Shoulder-wing, with swept leading edge mounted at rear. Large
winglets. Cylindrical composite fuselage with
pusher engine at rear. Canard
foreplane mounted high on long
pointed nose. One-piece canopy over
tandem seating. Main wheels fixed
but nosewheel retracts.

*Variants:* The Cozy was developed as a
side-by-side version of the Long-Ez.

**Above: Rutan Varieze. *PRM***

**Right: Rutan Long-Ez. *PRM***

**Scheibe SF-25 Falke.** *DJM*

# Scheibe SF-25 Falke
Two-seat powered sailplane
Basic data for Scheibe SF-25C
*Powerplant:* One 65hp (44.5kW) Limbach L1700A piston engine
*Span:* 50ft 2in (15.30m)
*Length:* 24ft 9in (7.55m)
*Max cruising speed:* 80mph (130km/h)
*Accommodation:* Two side-by-side seats
*First aircraft flown:* May 1963 (SF-25A); March 1971 (SF-25C)
*Production:* 1,031
*Recognition:* Single nose-engine-powered low-wing sailplane with high-aspect
ratio wings with marked dihedral and square tips. Very short nose. Square-
topped fin and rudder. Single-wheel, non-retractable, faired main
undercarriage with wing outriggers.
*Variants:* **SF-25A Motor Falke** — with 30hp (22.4kW) Hirth F12A2C engine;
**SF-25B Falke** — lower-set wings of reduced span and 45hp (33.5kW) Stamo
engine; **SF-25C Falke 76** — SF-25C with swept tail and clear blown
canopy; SF-**25C-200 Falke** — Falke 76 with 80hp (45.3kW) Limbach L2000-EA
engine and optional tricycle undercarriage; **SF-25K K-Falke** — SF-25C with
folding wings, larger canopy and GRP forward fuselage covering; **SF-25D
Falke** — SF-25B with Limbach engine; **Slingsby T61A Falke** — licence-built
by Slingsby Sailplanes; **SF-25E Super Falke** — has extended wing, air brakes,
narrow chord swept vertical tail, raised bubble canopy; **SF-28A/B Tandem
Falke** — Tandem two-seat version of SF-25C.

## SIPA S.903

Single-engined two-seat light aircraft
Basic data for SIPA S.903
*Powerplant:* One 90hp (67.1kW) Continental C90-8F piston engine
*Span:* 28ft 8in (8.73m)
*Length:* 18ft 10.5in (5.75m)
*Max cruising speed:* 109mph (175km/h)
*Accommodation:* Two side-by-side
*First aircraft flown:* 15 June 1947
*Production:* Some 113 were produced, with a variety of engines
*Recognition:* Single-engine low-wing monoplane. Short squat fuselage. Single-piece sliding canopy. Curved fin and rudder. Non-retractable tailwheel landing gear.
*Variants:* **S.90, S.901, S.902, S.904, S.91, S.92, S.93** and **S.94** were variants with different engines and/or different coverings for wings and fuselage.

*Above and left:* SIPA S.903. *PRM*

## Slingsby T67/T67M Firefly

Single-engined two-seat basic trainer
Basic data for Slingsby T67M MkII Firefly 200
*Powerplant:* One 160hp (119kW) Lycoming AEIO-320-D1B piston engine
*Span:* 34ft 9in (10.59m)
*Length:* 23ft 0in (7.01m)
*Max cruising speed:* 147mph (237km/h)
*Accommodation:* Two side-by-side seats
*First aircraft flown:* 15 May 1981 (T67A)
*Production:* 160+
*Recognition:* Single-engined low-wing glass reinforced plastic monoplane. Tapered wings with square tips. Fixed tricycle undercarriage without wheel spats. Large one-piece canopy. Square-topped fin and rudder with small dorsal fairing. Tailplane set on top of fuselage.
*Variants:* **T67A** — developed version of Fournier RF-6B under licence; **T67B** — T67A re-engineered in GRP with wider fuselage; **T67C** — powered by 160hp (119.3kW) engine; **T67D** — T67C with constant-speed propeller; **T67M** — with military equipment; **T67M-200** — 200hp (149.1kW) Lycoming AEIO-360-A1E and three-bladed propeller; **T67M-260** — two-seat military basic trainer, with 260hp (193.9kW) Lycoming AE10-540-D4A5 engine, supplied to USAF.

*Right:* **Slingsby T67M Firefly II.** *PRM*

*Below:* **Slingsby T67M Firefly 160.** *PRM*

## SOCATA (Gardan) GY-80 Horizon

Single-engined four-seat light aircraft
Basic data for Socata GY-80 Horizon
*Powerplant:* One 160hp (119kW) Lycoming O-320-B or 180hp (134kW) O-360-3A piston engine
*Span:* 31ft 10in (9.70m)
*Length:* 21ft 9in (6.64m)
*Max cruising speed:* 143mph (230km/h)
*Accommodation:* Pilot plus three passengers
*First aircraft flown:* 21 July 1960
*Production:* 267
*Recognition:* Single-engined low-wing monoplane with retractable tricycle undercarriage. Straight leading edge to wing with fillet at front wing root. Square wingtips. Short nose. Domed unglazed cockpit roof. Swept fin and rudder with small dorsal fairing.
*Variants:* Built in six basic versions. Standard versions have 150hp (114.5kW), 160hp (119.3kW) or 180hp (134.2kW) engines with fixed-pitch propellers, constant-speed propellers are optional equipment. The GY-80 design was developed into the ST-10 Super Horizon 200.

*Above:* **SOCATA/Gardan GY-80-160 Horizon.** *DJM*

*Right:* **SOCATA/Gardan GY-80-180 Horizon.** *DJM*

## SOCATA TB-9 Tampico/TB-10 Tobago/TB-20 Trinidad

Single-engined four-seat light aircraft
Basic data for Socata TB-10 Tobago
*Powerplant:* One 180hp (134.2kW) Lycoming O-320-A1AD piston engine
*Span:* 32ft 0in (9.76m)
*Length:* 25ft 3in (7.0m)
*Max cruising speed:* 146mph (235km/h)
*Accommodation:* Pilot plus three passengers
*First aircraft flown:* 23 February 1977 (TB-10); 9 March 1979 (TB-9);
   14 November 1980 (TB-20)
*Production:* 1,250+
*Recognition:* Single-engined low-wing monoplane. Wings of constant chord
   with square tips. Fixed tricycle undercarriage with large wheel spats. Tall
   swept fin and rudder with oblong tailplane set at pointed rear. Two
   side windows.
*Variants:* **TB-9 Tampico** — with 160hp (119.3kW) Lycoming O-320-D2A; **TB-9
   Club** — reduced specification for club training; **TB-10 Tobago** — more
   powerful 180hp (134.2kW) Lycoming O-360-A1AD; **TB-20 Trinidad** — TB-10
   with retractable undercarriage and 250hp (186.4kW) Lycoming IO-540-
   C4D5D; **TB-21 Trinidad TC** — TB-20 with turbocharged TIO-540-AB1AD
   engine; **TB200 Tobago XL** — with 200hp (149.1kW) Textron Lycoming
   IO-360-A1B6 first flew March 1991.

*Above:* SOCATA TB-20 Trinidad. *PRM*

*Right:* SOCATA TB-10 Tobago. *PRM*

## Stampe SV-4A/B/C/L

Single-engined two-seat aerobatic
and utility biplane.
Basic data for Stampe SV-4C
*Powerplant:* One 140hp (104kW)
   Renault 4 Pei piston engine
*Span:* 27ft 6in (8.38m)
*Length:* 22ft 10in (6.96m)
*Max cruising speed:* 109mph (175km/h)
*Accommodation:* Two seats in tandem
*First aircraft flown:* 17 May 1933
*Production:* 916 (post-1945)

*Top:* **Stampe SV-4B.** *PRM*

*Above:* **Stampe SV-4C.** *DJM*

*Recognition:* Single-engine biplane with slightly swept lower and upper wings
   of equal length. Rounded tips with ailerons on both wings. Fixed tail-dragger
   undercarriage with cross bracings on struts. Rounded fin and rudder.
   Rounded tailplane with cut-out at base. Twin open cockpits.
*Variants:* **SV-4** — original and wood fabric biplane powered by one 120hp
   (89.5kW) DH Gipsy III engine; **SV-4A** — SCAN-built with Renault 4P-05
   engine; **SV-4B** — SV-4A with 130hp (96.9kW) Gipsy Major engine and
   normally fitted with cockpit canopy, production by Stampe and Renard and
   SCAN; **SV-4C** — 140hp (104.4kW) Renault-engined version; **SV-4D** — SV-4C
   with 165hp (123.0kW) Continental IO-340-A engine; **SV-4E** — Lycoming
   engine.

## Stoddard-Hamilton Glasair III
Single-engined, two-seat dual control homebuilt aircraft
Basic data for Glasair III
*Powerplant:* One 300hp (224kW) Textron Lycoming IO-540-K1H5 piston engine.
   A turbocharged TIO-540 is an option
*Span:* 23ft 3.5in (7.10m)
*Length:* 21ft 4.75in (6.52m)
*Max cruising speed:* 280mph (451km/h)
*Accommodation:* Two, side-by-side
*First aircraft flown:* 1987
*Production:* Plans and kits available
*Recognition:* Single-engined, low-wing monoplane of glass-fibre and composite
   construction. Very sleek lines. Retractable tricycle undercarriage. Large
   cockpit canopy with glazed area behind pilot. Swept leading edge to fin and
   rudder, with small dorsal fillet. Small tailplane set on sloping rear fuselage.
   Prominent trim tab on rudder trailing edge.
*Variants:* The original version **Glasair II-S** replaced by the III in 1987; also a
   stretched version of the II-S. The II-FT and TD (fixed nosewheel and taildragger respectively) was first flown in 1979 and claimed as the first pre-
   moulded composite kitplane. The **Turbine 250/III,** developed in association
   with Becktold Aircraft, has a 450hp (335.6kW) Allison 250 turboprop.

**Left: Stoddard-Hamilton Glasair IIRG.** *PRM*

**Below: Stoddard-Hamilton Glasair III.** *PRM*

## Sukhoi Su-26, Su-29, Su-31

Basic date for Sukhoi Su-26MX
Single-seat aerobatic competition aircraft
*Powerplant:* One 360hp (268kW) Vedeneyev M-14P nine-cylinder radial engine
*Span:* 25ft 7in (7.80m)
*Length:* 22ft 5½in (6.84m)
*Max cruising speed:* 161mph (260km/h)
*Accommodation:* Pilot only (Su-26 and 31); pilot plus passenger, in
tandem (Su-29)
*First aircraft flown:* June 1984 (Su-26); late 1991 (Su-29); 1992 (Su-31)
*Recognition:* Mid-wing monoplane of specially developed symmetrical section,
variable along span. Long nose housing large radial engine, with three-blade
propeller. Straight under fuselage and upper fuselage drops sharply to rear
of cockpit canopy (single on Su-26 and Su-31, but double on Su-29). Sharp-
cornered (rather than rounded) fin and rudder. Non-retractable tailwheel
undercarriage. Arched cantilever mainwheel legs. Steerable tailwheel, on
long spring, connected to the rudder.
*Variants:* **Su-26M** — the basic model with **Su-26MX** (X for export) for the
export market; **Su-29** — the two-seat development of the Su-26MX with
wing span and overall length
increased; **Su-31** — a more advanced
single-seat version with a 400hp
(298kW) engine and has retractable
tailwheel.

*Above:* **Sukhoi Su-26MX.** *PRM*

*Right:* **Sukhoi Su-31.** *PRM*

# Tipsy Nipper

Single-engined single-seat ultra-light aerobatic aircraft
Basic data for Slingsby Nipper MkIII

*Powerplant:* One 55hp (41kW) Rollason-Ardem XI 1,500cc conversion of the Volkswagen piston engine
*Span:* 20ft 6in (6.25m)
*Length:* 15ft 0in (4.57m)
*Max cruising speed:* 93mph (150km/h)
*Accommodation:* Single-seat
*First aircraft flown:* 2 December 1957
*Production:* 117

*Recognition:* Single-engined shoulder-wing monoplane. Short fuselage with single-piece canopy above wings. Built-up rear fuselage. Fixed tricycle undercarriage. Main wheels on V-struts. Rectangular tail with square-topped fin and rudder. Wingtip tanks sometimes fitted.

*Variants:* **T66 Nipper Mk 1** — initial version produced by Avions·Fairey in Belgium with 40hp (29.8kW) Pollmann Hepu engine; **Nipper Mk2** — with 45hp (33.5kW) Stark Stamo 1400A engine built by Avions Fairey and other Belgian manufacturers; **Nipper Mk 3** — built by Slingsby at Kirkbymoorside; **Nipper Mk 3A** — optional 55hp (41.0kW) 1,600cc Ardem engine; **Nipper Mk 3B** — with 55hp (41.0kW) engine, more roomy cockpit and optional wingtip tanks.

*Right and below:* Tipsy Nipper T66 RA.45 Srs 3. *PRM*

# Van's RV-6

Single-engined, two-seat sporting homebuilt aircraft
Basic data for Van's RV-6
*Powerplant:* One 150-180hp (112-134kW) Textron Lycoming
   O-320 piston engine
*Span:* 23ft 0in (7.01m)
*Length:* 19ft 11in (6.07m)
*Max cruising speed:* 168mph (270 km/h)
*Accommodation:* Two, side-by-side
*First aircraft flown:* July 1988
*Production:* Plans and kits available
*Recognition:* Single-engined low-wing monoplane built of light alloy with
   glass-fibre wings. Non-retractable tailwheel landing gear. Large spats to main
   wheels. Upright fin and rudder. Tailplane set on top of sloping rear fuselage.
*Variants:* **RV-4** — first flew in June 1986, was developed from the
   RV-3 and was the fore-runner of the RV-6; **RV-6A** — a tricycle-landing-
   gear variation of the RV-6. It is built commercially in Nigeria as the Air Beetle.

*Above and left:* Van's RV-6. *PRM*

# Wittman Tailwind

Single-engined two-seat cabin homebuilt aircraft
Basic data for Wittman Tailwind Model W-8
*Powerplant:* Normally one 90hp (67kW) Teledyne Continental C90-12F piston
  engine. Numerous alternative engines
*Span:* 22ft 6in (6.86m)
*Length:* 19ft 3in (5.87m)
*Max cruising speed:* 130mph (209km/h)
*Accommodation:* Two, side-by-side
*First aircraft flown:* 1953
*Production:* Plans and kits available
*Recognition:* Single-engined high-wing monoplane. Single strut from lower
  fuselage to wing. Upper rear fuselage deck slopes steeply to tailfin. Non-
  retractable tailwheel landing gear. Slender mainwheel struts slightly stagger
  to rear. Angular fin and rudder with square top.
*Variants:* **Model W-10** is basically a W-8 with a 150hp (112kW) Textron
  Lycoming O-320, 145hp (108kW) Teledyne Continental — or aluminium block
  Oldsmobile F85 or Buick V-8 3,500cc (93kW) car engines.

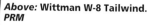

*Above:* **Wittman W-8 Tailwind.**
*PRM*

*Left:* **AJEP/Wittman W-8**
**Tailwind.** *PRM*

# Yakovlev Yak-52

Tandem two-seat primary trainer
Basic data for Yakovlev Yak-52
*Powerplant:* One 360hp (268kW) VMKB (Vedeneyev) M-14P nine-cylinder radial
  piston engine
*Span:* 30ft 6¹/₄in (9.30m)
*Length:* 25ft 5in (7.45m)
*Max cruising speed:* 167mph (270km/h)
*Accommodation:* Pilot plus one passenger
*First aircraft flown:* May 1978
*Production:* Approximately 1,600 (mainly for former USSR and Romanian
  Air Force)
*Recognition:* Low-wing monoplane with straight-tapered wings. Large
  'glasshouse' canopy. Semi-retractable tricycle undercarriage to reduce
  damage in a wheels-up landing. Large radial engine with louvres in front of
  cowling to regulate cooling. Large curved fin and rudder. Separate rearward
  sliding hood over each seat.
*Variants:* **Iak-52** — a licence version of the Soviet Yak-52 built by Aerostar SA
  (formerly IAV Bacau) in Romania; **Yak-50** and
  **53** — single-seat versions, with
  tailwheel and tricycle undercarriages
  respectively.

*Above:* **Yakovlev Yak-50.** *PRM*

*Right:* **Yakovlev Yak-52.** *PRM*

## Zlin 326/526/726

Single-engined aerobatic monoplane and utility aircraft
Basic data for Zlin 526F
*Powerplant:* One 180hp (134kW) Avia M137A piston engine
*Span:* 34ft 9in (10.60m)
*Length:* 26ft 3in (8.00m)
*Max cruising speed:* 130mph (210km/h)
*Accommodation:* Two seats in tandem
*First aircraft flown:* 20 October 1947 (Z-26); 12 August 1957 (Z-326);
   3 September 1965 (Z-526); 22 August 1973 (Z-726)
*Production:* 1,493
*Recognition:* Low-wing monoplane with swept leading-edge wing and straight
   trailing edge. Long nose. Semi-retractable main wheels, fixed tailwheel.
   Glazed canopy over tandem cockpit. Upright fin and rudder with small dorsal
   fairing from rear cabin. Square tips to tailplane with cut-out on trailing edge.
*Variants:* **Z-326 Trener Master; Z-526 Trener Master** — Z-326 with Avia V503
   propeller and rear seat moved back. Has pilot's seat at rear; **Z-326A** and
   **Z-526A Akrobat** — single-seat aerobatic versions; **Z-526L** — has 200hp
   (149.1kW) Lycoming AIO-360-B1B engine; **Z-726** — with 180hp (134.2kW)
   M137AZ engine; **Z-726K Universal** — with 210hp (156.6kW) M337AK
   supercharged engine.

**Right and below:** Zlin Z-326 Trener
Master. *PRM/APM*

*Above:*
**Westland-Bell 47G-4A.** *PRM*

*Left:*
**Bell 47G-381.** *PRM*

# Bell 47 Sioux

Light civil helicopter
Basic data for Bell 47G-3B
*Powerplant:* One 270hp (201.5kW) Lycoming TVO-435-F1A piston engine
*Main rotor diameter:* 37ft 2in (11.32m)
*Length:* 31ft 7in (9.63m)
*Max cruising speed:* 84mph (135km/h)
*Accommodation:* Pilot plus two passengers
*First aircraft flown:* 8 December 1945
*Production:* 2,197 built for US Army and over 1,000 by other manufacturers
*Recognition:* Goldfish-bowl cabin and tubular open tail-boom. Twin-blade main
    and rear rotors. Exposed engine to rear of cabin. Fixed-skid undercarriage.
*Variants:* Westland-built **Sioux AH1** helicopters were based on the civil Bell
    47G-3B-1. Many of these have come on the civil market and are used for
    light training and general purposes. A Bell 47 turbine with 313kW Allison
    250-20B conversion is produced by Soloy.

## Brantly B2

Single-engined light utility helicopter
Basic data for Brantly B2
*Powerplant:* One 180hp Lycoming IVO-360-A1A piston engine
*Main rotor diameter:* 23ft 9in (7.24m)
*Length:* 21ft 9in (6.62m)
*Max cruising speed:* 90mph (145Km/h)
*Accommodation:* Pilot plus one passenger
*First aircraft flown:* B2 — 21 February 1953
*Production:* Remained in production until 1982
*Recognition:* Large bulbous glazed nose with tapering fuselage to the rear
    extremity that has a small vertical fin. Enclosed engine. Three-blade main
    rotor and small two-blade tail rotor that is set on top of the port side of the
    tail fin. Very small horizontal tail stabilators of equal span. Skid
    undercarriage, with small retractable wheels at rear for ground handling.
*Variant:* **Brantly B305** — a larger four-seat version.

*Above and left:*
**Brantly B2B.** *PRM*

# Enstrom F.28/F.280C Shark

*Above:* **Enstrom 280C Shark.** *PRM*

Lightweight civil helicopter
Basic data for Enstrom F.280C Shark
*Powerplant:* One 205hp (153.0kW) Lycoming HIO-360-E1BD piston engine
*Main rotor diameter:* 32ft 0in (9.75m)
*Length:* 29ft 4in (8.94m)
*Max cruising speed:* 100mph (161km/h)
*Accommodation:* Pilot plus two passengers
*First aircraft flown:* 12 November 1960
*Production:* F.28A — 311; F.280C continues in production
*Recognition:* Large bulbous glazed nose with curved underfuselage. Skid
   undercarriage. Three-bladed main rotor set on tall single spindle. Small
   twin-bladed tail rotor set on starboard side. Small ventral tail which acts as
   guard/skid for rotor. Very small tailplane set well aft.
*Variants:* **F.28A** — original version; **F.28C** — with
   turbocharged Lycoming engine;
   **280 Shark** — more
   aerodynamically-shaped cabin
   and revised tail surfaces;
   **280C/280F/280FX Hawk** —
   further revisions of the Hawk;
   **F.28F Falcon** — with 225hp
   (167.8kW) Lycoming HIO-360-
   F1AD; **F.28F-P Sentinel** — the
   police variant.

*Right:* **Enstrom F.28F.** *PRM*

85

# Hughes 269/Schweizer 300

Commercial light helicopter
Basic data for Schweizer
269 Model 300C

*Powerplant:* One 190hp (141.8kW) Lycoming HIO-360-D1A piston engine

*Main rotor diameter:* 26ft 10in (8.18m)

*Length:* 22ft 0in (6.80m)

*Max cruising speed:* 99mph (159km/h)

*Above and below:*
**Hughes 269C.** *PRM/DJM*

*Accommodation:* Pilot plus two passengers; two seats in TH-55A

*First aircraft flown:* October 1956 (269); 1964 (300); June 1984 (300C)

*Production:* Hughes 269A — 1,200; 300C — production continues

*Recognition:* 'Wasp eye' glazed cabin with oval side doors. Exposed engine at lower rear of cabin. Twin skid undercarriage. Three-bladed main rotor on short main shaft. Thin tube rear fuselage with ventral brace. Small ventral V-shaped fin and starboard tailplane at 45°. Two-blade tail rotor on left of fuselage extremity. Curved skid at rear to protect rotor.

*Variants:* **Hughes 269A** — main production model; **TH-55A Osage** — US Army light helicopter primary trainer version; **300C** — current production version produced by Schweizer. Can be fitted with Allison 250-C20W turbine; **300CQ** — 'quiet' version; **300CB** — a new training helicopter; **330** — a turbine helicopter development with a 420shp (313.3kW) Allison 250-C20W turboshaft.

# Robinson R-22

**Above and below:**
**Robinson R-22 Beta.** *PRM*

Light utility and pilot-training helicopter
Basic data for Robinson R-22 Beta
*Powerplant:* One 160hp (119kW) Lycoming O-320-B2C piston engine
*Main rotor diameter:* 25ft 2in (7.67m)
*Length:* 28ft 9in (8.76m)
*Max cruising speed:* 110mph (177km/h)
*Accommodation:* Pilot plus one passenger/student
*First aircraft flown:* 28 August 1975
*Production:* 2,200+
*Recognition:* Small cabin with large glazed nose area. Twin side doors with
    windows. Faired main rotor head with twin-bladed main rotor. Enclosed
    engine. Tubular rear fuselage from upper rear of cabin. Small dorsal and
    ventral fin at fuselage extremity. Two-bladed rear rotor on port side.
    *Variants:* **R-22** — original model; **R-22 Alpha** — improved R-22; **R-22 Beta**
    — current production model with higher-powered
    Lycoming O-320-B2C; **R-22 Mariner** — float version;
    **R-22 IFR** — equipped with
    flight instruments for
    helicopter IFR training; **R-22 Agriculture** — equipped with
    spray system.

# Robinson R-44 Astro

Light utility and pilot-training helicopter

Basic data for Robinson R-44

*Powerplant:* One 260hp (193.8kW) Lycoming O-540 piston engine

*Main rotor diameter:* 33ft 0in (10.06m)

*Length:* 29ft 9in (9.07m)

*Max cruising speed:* 130mph (209km/h)

*Accommodation:* Pilot plus two passengers

*First aircraft flown:* 31 March 1990

*Production:* Over 250 operating in 20 countries mid-1996

*Recognition:* Basically a four-seat development of the R-22. Longer cabin with large glazed nose area and two windows on each side. Faired main rotor head with twin-bladed main rotor. Fully enclosed engine. Tubular rear fuselage from upper rear of cabin. Small dorsal and ventral fin at fuselage extremity. Two-bladed rear rotor on port side, with long curved rotor guard.

*Variants:* None

**Right and below:**
**Robinson R-44 Astro.** *PRM*

## Aero Designs Pulsar XP

Single-engined two-seat light homebuilt aircraft
*Powerplant:* One 80hp (59.7kW) Rotax 912 piston engine
*Span:* 25ft 0in (7.62m)
*Length:* 19ft 6in (5.94m)
*Max cruising speed:* 140mph (225km/h)
*Accommodation:* Two, side-by-side
*First aircraft flown:* 3 April 1988
*Production:* Over 200 kits have been delivered
*Variants:* The lighter weight **Pulsar** has a 66hp (49.2kW) Rotax 582 engine with
    a maximum cruising speed of 140mph (225km/h). This is a two-seat
    version of the Star-Lite.

**Right: Aero Designs
Pulsar XP.** *PRM*

**Left: Aviamilano F.8L
Falco I.** *PRM*

## Aviamilano F.8L Falco

Single-engined two-seat light aircraft
*Powerplant:* One 160hp (119.4kW) Lycoming O-320-B3B piston engine
*Span:* 26ft 3in (8.00m)
*Length:* 21ft 4in (6.50m)
*Max cruising speed:* 190mph (306km/h)
*Accommodation:* Two seats, side-by-side
*First aircraft flown:* 1955
*Production:* 60+; also manufactured by Aeromere, Laverda and kits by Sequoia

## Avid Aircraft Avid Flyer

Single-engined two-seat light homebuilt aircraft
*Powerplant:* One 65hp (48.5kW) Rotax 582 piston engine
*Span:* 29ft 10.5in (9.11m)
*Length:* 17ft 11in (5.46m)
*Max cruising speed:* 90mph (145km/h)
*Accommodation:* Two, side-by-side
*First aircraft flown:* 1983
*Production:* Plans and kits available
*Variants:* Optional floats, skis and wheel-skis. **Avid Commuter** has Rotax 582 CDI engine and has Aerobatic-Speedwings as standard. The **Avid Amphibian** (first flown 12 July 1985) is a three-seat amphibian. Wire-braced tail unit. **Avid Aerobat** is a two-seater, with a heavier empty weight and improved performance. **Aerobatic-Speedwings** has a shorter wingspan (23ft 11.5in – 7.30m) using a new wing section.

*Above:* Light Aero Avid Speed Wing Mk4. *PRM*

*Left:* Beagle A.61 Terrier. *PRM*

## Beagle A.61 Terrier

Single-engined high-wing aircraft
*Powerplant:* One 145hp (108.2kW) de Havilland Gipsy Major 10 Mk 1-1 piston engine
*Span:* 36ft 0in (10.97m)
*Length:* 23ft 8in (7.21m)
*Max cruising speed:* 115mph (185km/h)
*Accommodation:* Pilot plus three passengers
*First aircraft flown:* 25 April 1961
*Production:* 65; converted from Auster AOP6/T7

*Left:* **Christen Eagle II.** *PRM*

## Christen Eagle II

Single-engined two-seat aerobatic biplane
*Powerplant:* One 200hp (149.2kW) Lycoming AEIO-360-A1D piston engine
*Span:* 20ft 0in (6.96m)
*Length:* 18ft 6in (5.64m)
*Max cruising speed:* 165mph (265km/h)
*Accommodation:* Two seats in tandem
*First aircraft flown:* February 1977
*Production:* Many kits supplied to homebuilders

## Clutton-Tabenor Fred

Single-seat amateur-built light aircraft Fred Series 2 (Flying Runabout
Experimental Design)
*Powerplant:* One 37½hp (27.9kW) Lawrance radial (a converted APU engine)
*Span:* 22ft 6in (6.86m)
*Length:* 17ft 6in (5.33m)
*Max cruising speed:* 85mph (137km/h)
*Accommodation:* Pilot only
*First aircraft flown:*
    3 November 1963

*Right:* **Clutton-Tabenor Fred Srs 2.** *PRM*

## Currie Wot

Single-seat light biplane
*Powerplant:* One 65hp (48.5kW) Walter Mikron III piston engine
*Span:* 22ft 1in (6.73m)
*Length:* 18ft 3¹/₂in (5.68m)
*Max cruising speed:* 90mph (145km/h)
*Accommodation:* Pilot only
*First aircraft flown:* 11 September 1958 (although two examples were
    built in 1938)

*Left:* **Currie Wot.** *DJM*

*Below:* **De Havilland
DH60G Gipsy Moth.** *PRM*

## De Havilland DH60G Gipsy Moth

Single-engined two-seat
biplane trainer
*Powerplant:* One 60hp
    (44.8kW) ADC Cirrus I,
85hp (63.4kW) Cirrus II, 90hp (67.1kW) Cirrus III or 105hp (78.3kW) Cirrus
    Hermes piston engine
*Span:* 30ft 0in (9.14m)
*Length:* 23ft 11in (7.30m)
*Max cruising speed:* 102mph (164km/h)
*Accommodation:* Two seats in tandem open cockpits
*First aircraft flown:* 22 February 1925 (DH60); June 1928 (DH60G);
    August 1928 (DH60M)
*Production:* 500
*Similar variants:* **DH60** original version; **DH60G Gipsy Moth;
    DH60M Metal Moth.**

# De Havilland DH80A Puss Moth

Single-engined three-seat high-wing monoplane
*Powerplant:* One 120hp (89.5kW) Gipsy III or one 130hp (97.0kW) Gipsy Major
 or one 147hp (109.7kW) Gipsy Major piston engine
*Span:* 36ft 9in (11.20m)
*Length:* 25ft 0in (7.62m)
*Max cruising speed:* 108mph
 (173.8km/h)
*Accommodation:* Pilot plus
 three passengers
*First aircraft flown:*
 9 September 1929
*Production:* 259 (England),
 25 (Canada)

**Above:** De Havilland
DH80A Puss Moth. *PRM*

**Left:** De Havilland
DH83C Fox Moth. *PRM*

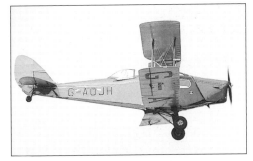

# De Havilland DH83 Fox Moth

Single-engined five-seat biplane
*Powerplant:* One 120hp (89.5kW) de Havilland Gipsy III, 130hp
 (97.0kW) Gipsy Major or 145hp (108.2kW) Gipsy
 Major 1C piston engine
*Span:* 30ft 10in (9.17m)
*Length:* 25ft 9in (7.85m)
*Max cruising speed:* 105mph (169.3km/h)
*Accommodation:* Pilot plus four passengers
*First aircraft flown:* 29 January 1932
*Production:* 146 (including Canadian and Australian production)
*Similar variants:* Canadian-built Fox Moths were designated **De
 Havilland DH83C** and featured pilot's canopy, some were float- or
 ski-equipped.

## De Havilland DH85 Leopard Moth

Single-engined light cabin aircraft
*Powerplant:* One 130hp (97.0kW) DH Gipsy Major I piston engine
*Span:* 37ft 6in (11.43m)
*Length:* 24ft 6in (7.47m)
*Max cruising speed:* 119mph (191km/h)
*Accommodation:* Pilot plus two passengers
*First aircraft flown:* 27 May 1933
*Production:* 132

**Right:** De Havilland DH85
Leopard Moth. **PRM**

## De Havilland DH87B Hornet Moth

Single-engined light cabin biplane
*Powerplant:* One 130hp (97.0kW) DH Gipsy Major I piston engine
*Span:* 31ft 11in (9.48in)
*Length:* 25ft 0in (7.63m)
*Max cruising speed:* 105mph (169km/h)
*Accommodation:* Pilot plus passenger in side-by-side seating
*First aircraft flown:* 9 May 1934
*Production:* 165

**Left:** De Havilland
DH87B Hornet Moth.
**BSS**

## De Havilland DH89A Dragon Rapide

Twin-engine light transport biplane
*Powerplant:* Two 200hp (149.3kW) de Havilland Gipsy Queen piston engines
*Span:* 48ft 0in (14.63m)
*Length:* 34ft 6in (10.51m)
*Max cruising speed:* 132mph (212km/h)
*Accommodation:* Pilot plus five/seven passengers
*First aircraft flown:* 17 April 1934
*Production:* 729

*Left:* **De Havilland DH89A Dragon Rapide.** *PRM*

*Right:* **De Havilland DH94 Moth Minor.** *DJM*

## De Havilland DH94 Moth Minor

Single-engined tandem-seat low-wing monoplane
*Powerplant:* One 80hp (59.5kW) de Havilland Gipsy Minor piston engine
*Span:* 36ft 7in (11.14m)
*Length:* 24ft 5in (7.45m)
*Max cruising speed:* 100mph (160.93km/h)
*Accommodation:* Pilot plus one passenger
*First aircraft flown:* 22 June 1937
*Production:* 100+
*Similar variants:* Built as tandem-seat open cockpit and as coupé version.

# Denney Aerocraft Kitfox

Two-seat dual-control homebuilt aircraft
*Powerplant:* One 65hp (48.5kW) Rotax 582LC piston engine, optional 80hp
  (59.7kW) Rotax 912
*Span:* 32ft 0in (9.75m)
*Length:* 17ft 8in (5.38m)
*Max cruising speed:* 105mph (169km/h)
*Accommodation:* Pilot plus one passenger
*First aircraft flown:* 7 May 1984
*Production:* Construction by amateur builders

*Left:* **Denney Aerocraft Kitfox 3.** *PRM*

# Erco Ercoupé/Forney Aircoupé

Two-seat single-engined cabin monoplane
*Powerplant:* Prewar — one 65hp (48.5kW) Continental A-65-8. Postwar — one
  75hp (55.97kW) Continental C-75-12 piston engine
*Span:* 30ft 0in (9.14m)
*Length:* 20ft 9in (6.32m)
*Max cruising speed:* 110mph (177.02km/h)
*Accommodation:* Pilot plus one passenger
*First aircraft flown:* October 1937 (Erco 310)
*Production:* Prewar — 112; postwar — 5,504
*Similar variants:* Known as Erco Ercoupé until April 1955 when it was taken over
  by the Forney Aircraft Manufacturing Co and became Forney Aircoupé.

*Right:* **Forney F1A Aircoupé.** *PRM*

# Evans VP-1/VP-2

Single-seat homebuilt light monoplane
*Powerplant:* One 40hp (30kW), 53hp
   (39.5kW) or 60hp (44.5kW)
   modified Volkswagen motorcar engine
*Span:* 24ft 0in (7.32m)
*Length:* 18ft 0in (5.49m)
*Max cruising speed:* 75mph
   (121km/h)
*Accommodation:* Pilot only
*Production:* Construction
   by amateur builders
*Variants:* **Evans VP-2** is a
   two-seat version.

*Above:* **Evans VP-1.** *PRM*

*Left:* **FFA AS202 Bravo.**

# FFA AS202 Bravo

Single-engined light training aircraft
*Powerplant:* One 180hp (134.3kW) AE10-360-B1F piston engine
*Span:* 32ft 0in (9.75m)
*Length:* 24ft 7in (7.50m)
*Max cruising speed:* 141mph (226km/h)
*Accommodation:* Two side-by-side seats
*First aircraft flown:* 7 March 1969
*Production:* 180

## Gardan (CAB) GY-20 Minicab

Single-engined low-wing light aircraft
*Powerplant:* One 65hp (48.5kW) Continental A-65-8 piston engine
*Span:* 26ft 8in (8.14m)
*Length:* 17ft 11in (5.46m)
*Max cruising speed:* 105mph (170km/h)
*Accommodation:* Two side-by-side seats
*First aircraft flown:* 1 February 1949
*Production:* 22 (plus 37 by amateur builders)
*Similar variants:*
**GY-30 Supercab.**

*Right:* **Hume/Gardan
GY-20 Minicab.** *PRM*

*Left:* **Isaacs Fury II.** *PRM*

## Isaacs Fury

Single-engined single-seat light biplane
*Powerplant:* One four-cylinder horizontally opposed air-cooled engine of
   90–125hp (67.1-93.2kW) or one 125hp (93.3kW) Lycoming O-290
   piston engine
*Span:* Top 21ft 0in (6.40m); bottom 18ft 2in (5.54m)
*Length:* 18ft 6in (5.64m)
*Max cruising speed:* 115mph (185km/h)
*Accommodation:* Pilot only in open cockpit
*First aircraft flown:* 30 August 1963 (Mk I); July 1967 (Mk II)
*Production:* Construction by amateur builders

*Left:* Jodel D.18. *PRM*

## Jodel D.18

Single-engined homebuilt low-wing monoplane
*Powerplant:* One 58hp (43kW) 1,600cc Volkswagen engine
*Span:* 24ft 7.25in (7.50m)
*Length:* 18ft 8.5in (5.70m)
*Max cruising speed:* 105mph (170km/h)
*Accommodation:* Pilot plus one passenger
*First aircraft flown:* 21 May 1984
*Production:* Construction by amateur builders
*Similar variants:* **Jodel D.19** is the D.18 with a tricycle landing gear.

*Right:* Luton LA4A
Minor. *PRM*

## Luton LA4 Minor

Single-seat ultra-light parasol monoplane
*Powerplant:* One 40hp (30kW) Aeronca JAP J-99; others optional
*Span:* 25ft 0in (7.62m)
*Length:* 20ft 0in (6.09m)
*Max cruising speed:* 75mph (120.7km/h)
*Accommodation:* Pilot only in open cockpit
*First aircraft flown:* 1938
*Production:* 25 + in UK by amateur builders

## Maule M-5/M-6/M-7

Four/five-seat high-wing light monoplane
*Powerplant:* One 210hp (156.5kW) Avco Lycoming TO-360-C1A 6D
   piston engine
*Span:* 30ft 10in (9.4m)
*Length:* 22ft 1in (6.71m)
*Max cruising speed:* 189mph (304km/h)
*Accommodation:* Pilot plus three passengers
*First aircraft flown:* 1 November 1971 (M-5)
*Production:* In excess of 1,800 of all variants have been built
*Similar variants:* The **M-5 Lunar Rocket** has larger tail surfaces and increased
   flap area. The five-seat **M-6 Super Rocket** was introduced in 1984. The
   current version is the **M-7-235 Super Rocket,** a long wingspan (33ft
   8in/10.26m) five-seater with either 235hp (175kW) Textron Lycoming O-540-
   J1A5D or IO-540-W1A5D engine. The **MX-7-180 Star Rocket** has the
   fuselage of the M-6 with the shorter span wing of the M-5; **M-7-420** — with
   420hp (313.2kW) Allison 250-B17C turboprop and Edo 2500 amphibious
   floats; **MXT-7-180** — new version with tricycle undercarriage.

*Left:* Maule M4-210C
Rocket. *PRM*

*Below:* MBB Bo.209
Monsun 150FF. *PRM*

## MBB Bo.209 Monsun

Single-engined light aircraft
*Powerplant:* One 150hp (111.9kW) Lycoming
   IO-320-E1C or 160hp (119.3kW)
   O-320-E1F piston engine
*Span:* 27ft 7in (8.40m)
*Length:* 21ft 7in (6.60m)
*Max cruising speed:* 155mph
   (250km/h)
*Accommodation:*
   Two side-by-side seats
*First aircraft flown:*
   22 December 1967
*Production:* 102

## Oldfield 'Baby' Lakes

Single-engined single-seat homebuilt sporting biplane

Basic data for Oldfield 'Baby' Lakes

*Powerplant:* One 85hp (63.4kW) Teledyne Continental piston engine. Provision for alternative engines of between 50 and 100hp (37.25 and 74.5kW)

*Span:* 16ft 8in (5.08m)

*Length:* 13ft 9in (4.19m)

*Max cruising speed:* 118mph (190km/h)

*Accommodation:* Pilot only

*First aircraft flown:* 1976

*Above:* **Oldfield 'Baby' Lakes.** *PRM*

*Production:* Construction by amateur builders

*Variants:* The **'Super Baby' Lakes** is a more powerful and modified variant with a 108hp (80.5kW) Textron Lycoming. The **'Buddy Baby' Lakes** is a two-seat version, for aerobatic training, with widened fuselage and a 125hp (93.2kW) Textron Lycoming O-320.

## Piper PA-15/17 Vagabond

Single-engined high-wing light aircraft

*Powerplant:* One 65hp (48.5kW) Continental A-65-8 piston engine (PA-17)

*Span:* 29ft 3in (8.91m)

*Length:* 18ft 8in (5.67m)

*Max cruising speed:* 92mph (148km/h)

*Accommodation:* Two side-by-side seats

*First aircraft flown:* 29 October 1947

*Production:* 601

*Variants:* The **PA-15** had single controls and a 65hp (48.5kW) Lycoming O-235 engine. The **PA-16 Clipper** is a PA-15 with an enlarged four-seat fuselage and 108hp (80.6kW) Lycoming O-235.

*Right:* **Piper PA-17 Vagabond.** *PRM*

## Piper PA-46-310P Malibu

Single-engined light pressurised-cabin aircraft
*Powerplant:* One 310hp (231.3kW) turbocharged Continental TSIO-520-BE piston engine
*Span:* 43ft 0in (13.11m)
*Length:* 28ft 5in (8.66m)
*Max cruising speed:* 248mph (400km/h)
*Accommodation:* Pilot plus five passengers
*First aircraft flown:* 30 November 1979
*Production:* 573
*Variants:* **PA-46-350P Malibu Mirage** — with 350hp (261.0kW) Lycoming TIO-540-AE2A.

*Right:* **Piper PA-46-310P Malibu.** *PRM*

*Below:* **Rand-Robinson KR-2.** *PRM*

## Rand-Robinson KR-2

Single-engined single-seat sporting homebuilt aircraft
Basic data for Rand-Robinson KR-2
*Powerplant:* Airframe designed to accept Volkswagen modified motorcar engines of 1,600 to 2,200cc
*Span:* 20ft 8in (6.30m)
*Length:* 14ft 6in (4.42m)
*Max cruising speed:* 180mph (290km/h)
*Accommodation:* Two, side-by-side
*First aircraft flown:* February 1972 (KR-1); July 1974 (KR-2)
*Production:* Plans and kits available
*Variants:* **KR-1** was the initial single-seat version and the **KR-1B** was the motor glider version with a span of 27ft (8.23m). The **KR-100** is an entirely new single-seat version with a Teledyne Continental O-200 engine. **KR-2S** has a 16in (0.41m) longer fuselage, higher canopy, 23ft (7m) span and a 76hp (56.7kW) VW engine.

*Left:* RANS S-10 Sakota.
*PRM*

*Below:* Jodel D.140C
Mousquetaire. *DJM*

## RANS S-10 Sakota

Single-engined two-seat homebuilt aircraft
Basic data for RANS S-10 Sakota
*Powerplant:* One 65hp (48.5kW) Rotax 582 piston engine, with 2.58:1 reduction
  gear standard. Optional 90hp (67kW) AMW 636
*Span:* 24ft 0in (7.32m)
*Length:* 17ft 10in (5.44m)
*Max cruising speed:* 100mph (161km/h)
*Accommodation:* Two, side-by-side
*Production:* Plans and kits available
*Variants:* **The RANS S-9 Chaos** was the original single-seat version of which
  the S-10 is basically a two-seat derivative. It has a 49.6hp (37kW) Rotax
  503SC engine.

## SAN/Jodel D.140 Mousquetaire

Single-engined four/five-seat touring aircraft
*Powerplant:* One 180hp (134.3kW) Lycoming O-360-A2A piston engine
*Span:* 38ft 8in (10.26m)
*Length:* 25ft 8in (7.82m)
*Max cruising speed:* 130mph (210km/h)
*Accommodation:* Pilot plus
  three/four passengers
*First aircraft flown:*
  4 July 1958 (D.140)
*Production:* 243 by SAN including
  D.140R Abeille (28)
*Variants:* **D.140A/B Mousquetaire
  I/II** — has triangular fin and
  rudder. **D.140C/E Mousquetaire
  III/IV** — larger, swept fins,
  modified engine cowling and
  tailplane; **D.140R Abeille** —
  cut-down rear fuselage.

## Steen Skybolt

Single-engined two-seat homebuilt aerobatic and sport biplane
*Powerplant:* One 260hp (194.0kW) Textron Lycoming IO-640-D4A5 piston engine. Alternative engines, including radials, from 160-350hp (119-261kW) acceptable
*Span:* Upper 24ft 0in (7.32m); lower 23ft 0in (7.01m)
*Length:* 19ft 0in (5.79m)
*Max cruising speed:* 160mph (257km/h)
*Accommodation:* Two in tandem
*First aircraft flown:* October 1970
*Production:* Plans and kits available
*Variants:* None. The design rights were purchased by Hale Wallace in 1990.

*Above:* **Steen Skybolt.** *PRM*

## Stolp Starduster Too/Acroduster

Single-engined two-seat light aircraft
*Powerplant:* 180hp (134kW) Lycoming O-360-A1A piston engine
*Span:* Upper 24ft 0in (7.32m); lower 20ft 5in (6.22m)
*Length:* 20ft 3in (6.17m)
*Max cruising speed:* 150mph (241km/h)
*Accommodation:* Pilot plus one passenger in tandem
*First aircraft flown:* 1 November 1957 (Starduster 1); late 1960s (Starduster Too)
*Production:* Plans were available for amateur constructors
*Similar variants:* **Stolp SA-300 Starduster Too** is the two-seat sporting biplane version. **Stolp SA-500** is a single-seat swept parasol-wing monoplane version. **Stolp SA-700 Acroduster 1** is a single-seat fully aerobatic biplane and **SA-750 Acroduster Too** is the two-seat aerobatic biplane. The original **Stolp-Adams SA-100 Starduster** had a 150hp (111.8kW) Lycoming O-320 engine.

*Right:* **Stolp SA-750 Acroduster Too.** *PRM*

# Taylorcraft BC-12D
Single-engined high-wing monoplane
*Powerplant:* One 85hp (63.4kW) Continental C-85 piston engine
*Span:* 36ft (10.97m)
*Length:* 21ft 10in (6.65m)
*Max cruising speed:* 95mph (153km/h)
*Accommodation:* Two side-by-side seats
*First aircraft flown:* 1938
*Similar variants:* **Taylorcraft A/BC/BC-65/Plus C/D, Auster 1**

*Left:* **Taylorcraft BC-12D.
PRM**

*Below:* **Taylor JT2 Titch.
DJM**

# Taylor Monoplane
Single-seat fully-aerobatic
monoplane
*Powerplant:* One 38hp (29kW)
  JAP two-cylinder engine;
  others optional
*Span:* 21ft 0in (6.40m)
*Length:* 15ft 0in (4.57m)
*Max cruising speed:*
  90mph (145km/h)
*Accommodation:* Pilot only
*First aircraft flown:*
  JT1 — 8 August1964;
  JT2 — 22 January 1967

*Production:* Constructed by amateur builders
*Similar variants:* **JT2 Titch** has an 85hp (63.4kW) Continental C85-12F engine
  with reduced wingspan of 18ft 9in (5.72m) but increased length of
  16ft 1.5in (4.91m).

## Victa AESL Airtourer

Single-engined light aircraft
*Powerplant:* One 150hp (111.9kW) Lycoming O-320-E2A piston engine
*Span:* 26ft 0in (7.92m)
*Length:* 21ft 6in (6.55m)
*Max cruising speed:* 140mph (225km/h)
*Accommodation:* Two side-by-side seats
*First aircraft flown:* 31 March 1959 (MkI)
*Production:* Victa 170; AESL 176 (including 96 military trainers)
*Similar variants:* **Airtourer T1-T6; AirtrainerCT4/CT4A/CT4B/C T4E.**

*Right:* **Victa AESL Airtourer 100.** *PRM*

## Yakovlev Yak-18/18T

Single-engined four-seat general-purpose cabin aircraft
*Powerplant:* One 300hp (224kW) Ivechenko AI-14RF nine-cylinder radial engine
*Span:* 36ft 7¼in (11.16m)
*Length:* 27ft 4¾in (8.35m)
*Max cruising speed:* 155mph (250km/h)
*Accommodation:* Pilot plus three passengers
*First aircraft flown:* Yak-18 — 1946; Yak-18T — 1967

*Above:* **Yakovlev Yak-18T**

*Similar variants:* **Yak-18** — was initial production version with tailwheel landing gear. **Yak-18U** — modified version of Yak-18 with tricycle undercarriage. **Yak-18A** — with enlarged cockpit and more powerful engine. **Yak-18P** — a single-seat development of Yak-18A for advanced training. **Yak-18PM** — a single-seat aerobatic version. **Yak-18T** — an extensively redesigned four-seat general-purpose cabin version, with increased span currently in production.

*Left:* **Zenair CH-601HD** Zodiac. *PRM*

# Zenair Zodiac CH-601

Single-engined two-seat homebuilt aircraft
*Powerplant:* One 80hp (59.7kW) Rotax 912 piston engine
*Span:* 23ft 0in (7.0m)
*Length:* 19ft 0in (5.79m)
*Max cruising speed:* 130mph (209km/h)
*Accommodation:* Two, side-by-side
*First aircraft flown:* June 1984 (CH-601); August 1991 (CH-601HDS)
*Production:* Plans and kits available
*Variants:* **Zenair Zodiac CH-601D** — the relaunched version of the CH-600 and is 85% preassembled. It has the wider cabin than the CH601; **Zenair Super Zodiac 601HDS** — a shorter span and tapered 'speed' wing. Optional engines include converted motorcar types.

# INDEX

# INDEX

**Left:**
**Steen Skybolt.** *PRM*

*Top:* **De Havilland DH89A Dragon Rapide.** *PRM*

*Above:* **Stolp SA.5300 Starduster Too.** *PRM*

*Right:* **Zenair CH-601HD Zodiac.** *PRM*